SHOPLIFTING AND SHRINKAGE PROTECTION FOR STORES

Shoplifting and Shrinkage Protection for Stores

Fifth Printing

By

LOREN E. EDWARDS

*Consultant on Inventory
Shrinkage Problems
Apple Valley, California*

*Formerly, Protection Manager
Marshall Field and Company
Chicago, Illinois*

CHARLES C THOMAS · PUBLISHER
Springfield · Illinois · U.S.A.

Published and Distributed Throughout the World by

CHARLES C THOMAS • PUBLISHER
BANNERSTONE HOUSE
301-327 East Lawrence Avenue, Springfield, Illinois, U.S.A.

This book is protected by copyright. No part of it may be reproduced in any manner without written permission from the publisher.

© *1958, by* CHARLES C THOMAS • PUBLISHER
ISBN 0-398-00498-6
Library of Congress Catalog Card Number: 58-14069

First Printing, 1958
Second Printing, 1970
Third Printing, 1972
Fourth Printing, 1974
Fifth Printing, 1976

With THOMAS BOOKS *careful attention is given to all details of manufacturing and design. It is the Publisher's desire to present books that are satisfactory as to their physical qualities and artistic possibilities and appropriate for their particular use.* THOMAS BOOKS *will be true to those laws of quality that assure a good name and good will.*

Printed in the United States of America

N-1

PREFACE

SHRINKAGE or loss is one of the controversial subjects of retailing, and shortage control is a problem of major proportions. It has frequently been the topic of discussion in forums and clinics on store protection. Articles on shrinkage, shoplifting, and employe thefts in trade papers, magazines, and newspapers have been legion, but I know of no publication available to store personnel and students of retailing that covers all of the protection problems of retailers. My aim is to give a brief account of situations faced by stores and to answer some questions that have frequently been asked.

A store executive once made the statement, "If we actually knew what is being stolen we would probably all lose our minds."

"We lose more money by stock shortage than we make." This statement, meaning that shrinkage was greater than profit, was made by a store comptroller at a comptrollers' meeting.

Another store comptroller made the statement that "shoplifting in stores comprises 30 per cent of all inventory shrinkage or loss." The theory has also been advanced that the major part of losses, due to theft, is caused by dishonest employes.

One expert in the field of shrinkage prevention has estimated that a fantastic sum of money—$1,700,000,000—is stolen from retailers each year. Another estimate was that approximately 100,000 thefts, at an average take of $15 each, are committed nationally each week. That figure would add up to $78,000,000 a year. In my opinion this is a very conservative figure.

Any actual loss figure for the nation can only be a guess, because it is impossible to determine the portion of shrinkage that is due to theft and that which is caused by errors or neglect.

One thing is certain; shrinkage affects small, medium-sized, and large stores, and a program for its control should have top priority with the management of all stores.

There can be no doubt that shrinkage is due both to theft and to errors or carelessness. Therefore, a reduction program cannot separate carelessness from crime but must embrace them both as preventive factors.

Most stores operate on the assumption that buyers of departments or managers of shops or specialty stores have the full responsibility for inventories. A protection department is usually considered as an agency to apprehend thieves. It should also assist the management in preventing or reducing shrinkage.

In recent years it has become more and more evident that store managements are realizing that protection is everybody's job. All department heads, accounting, protection, and all employes should be kept informed of the problems.

I recommend that every store conduct regular and repeated educational programs, for all employes of the store, covering the loss problems, and emphasizing the need for constant vigilance by everyone.

During 22 years, while managing the protection department of one large Chicago store, I have handled or been closely associated with some 30,000 theft cases. I had devoted myself to a shrinkage reduction program with some measure of success, yet I do not have all the answers to all the problems.

I do hope that some of my experiences and studies may help some store managements in that educational program which I recommend; that it may help to stress the difficulties encountered by store protection agents and promote greater appreciation of their efforts; and also that it may help to serve as a factor to deter thefts from within.

So many different individuals have contributed to my knowledge of protection, and aided in my experiences, that I cannot acknowledge recognition of each one. I am grateful to every person who has worked with me in protection over the years. I have benefited from the association with each and every one.

The assistance of many co-workers throughout the store, in every branch of the business, and their interest in my operation has been greatly appreciated. Many conversations, suggestions, and tips from them have helped me to handle thousands of the many cases similar to these:

Preface

The buyer who "blew her top" when she thought someone had forged her name to a refund was responsible for my first large case many years ago. It developed that her name had been forged and the forger had imitated the signature of other buyers to the extent of some $20,000.

I admired the keen perception of a young exchange clerk who, when placed in a new location, was reluctant to question the authority of a section supervisor, but did make a record of questionable transactions. When it seemed advisable for her to report to her supervisor, a series of thefts covering a period of many years was brought to a conclusion.

I regret being unable to personally thank persons for anonymous information that has proven to be authentic, especially one of the more recent cases where a group of employes was involved.

I appreciate the cooperation I have received from protection personnel of other stores and from many law enforcement officers. Prosecuters, judges, and lawyers have constantly contributed to my knowledge.

I also wish to acknowledge my appreciation to those culprits who have cooperated so fully upon being apprehended. In some instances information given by them, involving risks, has been used to help further security.

ACKNOWLEDGMENTS

From the beginning of my career in store protection I have maintained a desire to fathom the enigmatic qualities of the persons and situations encountered. Many notes were made in the hope that some day I would discover some of the answers.

Friends had often commented that I should write a book on my experiences, but the inception of the manuscript was due to the suggestion, encouragement, and enthusiasm of John Richelieu Davis, Lecturer in Industrial Security, Michigan State University; Security Co-ordinator, The Hallicrafters Company; Director, Davis Associates, Plant Protection Consultants, Chicago. Many thanks to him. I have enjoyed and benefited from the work and effort put into it.

I appreciate the authorization I received from my superior to work with Mary Owen Cameron in her study of "Department Store Shoplifting." In the acknowledgment in her thesis she states, "The aid given to the writer by the Protection Department is obvious in every page of this study, but the appreciation of the need for basic research in criminology that the store officials expressed is not elsewhere acknowledged." In turn, may I acknowledge the usefulness of Dr. Cameron's study and express my sincere appreciation for her letter:

> You certainly have my permission to use any parts of my dissertation that may seem useful to you.
>
> I have been away from the details of work involved in preparing the dissertation long enough to ask myself—what, if anything, did I find that is of significance? And it seems to me that there is at least one point that needs a good deal more exploration. This is the fact that so very few people who were handled by the store protection staff had any previous record. Once arrested, pilferers were "cured." (See pages 172-174 of the dissertation.)
>
> From the general point of criminology this is a very significant fact, and an understanding of the why's and how's of it might be

ix

important to our total treatment program for first offenders. The store protection staff was, in other words, more effectively "curing" offenders than courts and penal institutions have ever been able to do. The fact that, in a sense, these were lesser offenders does not seem to me to be the major answer.

I feel that the answer is deeper than this. The pilferer (who may well have been stealing for years without being caught) when picked up by the store detectives was forced for the first time to consider himself as a "low down, no good thief." The scorn and contempt with which the store detectives treated him came as a tremendous shock. Furthermore in the store arrest he (or she) did not encounter people who could or would aid him in building up ego-saving rationalizations.

There is undoubtedly more to the situation than this, but anyway it seems clear to me that your store protection staff has arrived at a most important and significant way of handling a first offender. If this process could be more thoroughly understood it might be of considerable importance in handling other kinds of first offenders. If you have any psychologist or psychiatrist acquaintances you might suggest this problem to them.

It certainly is a problem I'd like to work on, but I carry too heavy a teaching schedule to allow time for research.

Cordially, _____ signed
Dr. Mary Owen Cameron

I am grateful to associates for their valued contributions, suggestions, and appraisement of parts or all of the manuscript. Many thanks to:

Mr. Arthur H. Hagen, Chief, Security Section, Jewel Tea Company.

Dr. Joseph W. Harney, Psychology Instructor, Wright Junior College.

Mr. Fred V. Hersey, Supervisor of Property Protection, Mandel Brothers

Dr. Lois Lundell Higgins, Director, Crime Prevention Bureau of Illinois.

Mr. Albert M. Howard, Trial Lawyer, Chicago.

Mr. Fred Inbau, Professor of Law, Northwestern University.

Mr. Paul W. Ligman, Chief Security Representative, National Tea Co.

Mr. Horace N. Lund, Lawyer and Assistant States Attorney, Cook County.

Mr. Lester W. Rank, Director of Protection, Carson Pirie Scott & Co.

Lt. Edward A. Stanwyck, Illinois State Police, Commanding C.I.U.

Dr. Richard C. Steinmetz, Chief Special Agent, Mutual Investigation Bureau.

Mr. C. Vernon Thompson, Trial Lawyer, Chicago.

Acknowledgments would not be complete without recognition of the time and patience of my sister, Retreva Edwards Dyer, for typing and retyping my writing, and to my niece, Kay Dyer Ostborg, for corrections.

L. E. E.
Post Office Box 383
Apple Valley, California

Chapter

7. PICKPOCKETS 72
   An account of the operations of "Pickpockets"; their "take"; and advice on prevention of losses.

8. NIMBLE FINGERS, MISCELLANEOUS 80
   Theft of purses—"Sleepers"; "Till-Tappers" thefts from cash registers; Thefts of employe "banks."

9. NARCOTICS AND ADDICTION 84
   "Addiction"—a peril to be reckoned with by all merchants.

10. JUVENILE PROBLEMS OF STORES 91
    Retail stores present temptation to youths, employes and the public. Education, prohibitions, and controls, are necessities for prevention of delinquency; Finesse advised in accosting thieves, both juvenile and adult, 93; Arson and investigation, 98-99.

11. NEIGHBORHOOD DEPARTMENT STORES 101
    The loss potential for smaller stores is equal to that for downtown stores. Shoplifters, professional and amateur, and employes, pose shrinkage problems.

12. CANDY—FOODS—SELF-SERVICE MARKETS 106
    The pilfering of foods is not considered as stealing by many persons, but does cause reduced profits; the prevention of loss and the apprehension of shoplifters is of vital importance in maintaining profits for food operations.

13. FRAUDULENT CHECKS—CHARGES—CONFIDENCE GAME 115
    Methods of operation and advice for prevention of losses due to fraudulent checks—charges—and con game; Removal of incriminating evidence from, upon or within, the body of accused persons, 120; Counterfeit money, 123.

14. HONESTY SHOPPING 125
    The temptation to salespeople handling cash necessitates "Honesty Shopping," or other methods for the prevention of loss.

15. RELEASE OR PROSECUTION 130
    Screening of shoplifters for release or prosecution. Amateur shoplifters often benefit from release, however, it is advisable to prosecute all "Professional Thieves," repeaters, and narcotic

Chapter

addicts; Shoplifters stealing merchandise at $20 or more, 132; Study of 709 adult women to determine previous records, 132; Method of making arrest to prevent excitement, 134; Advice for handling of juveniles, 136; Problems of civil false arrest suits follow failure to obtain guilty verdicts of criminal charges, 137-138.

16. STORE DETECTIVES ARE HUMAN 139
    Protection personnel face temptations.

17. COOPERATION WITH OTHER AGENCIES 146
    Store personnel can solve crimes by cooperation with all other local law enforcement agencies; A study of shoplifters with merchandise from other stores at the time of their arrest is a recommendation for cooperation between all local stores, 150.

18. PROTECTION TASKS ARE KALEIDOSCOPIC 151
    Lost children and persons, 151-152; Lost articles, 152; Runaway children, 153; Identification of handwriting, 153; Deranged persons, 153-155; Intoxicated persons, 155; Fire and accident prevention, 155; Arson, 156; Insurance protection, 156-159; Guards and watchmen, 159-160; Emergency illnesses or other crises, 160.

19. ROBBERY—BURGLARY 161
    A possibility for any store. Employes need instructions in actions to be taken.

20. LOCKS—ALARMS—PLANTS 165
    A brief discussion on protective measures, primarily useful during closing hours.

21. WATCHDOGS 171
    Dogs can assist in protection of property.

22. SHOPLIFTING LAWS—PENALTIES 176
    A discussion of laws and penalties of several different states intended to impress merchants with the importance of determining legal rights as interpreted locally; Discussion on false arrest or false imprisonment.

23. INVESTIGATION 183
    Books have been devoted to the subject of investigation; Points on various types of investigation helpful in protection of stores.

Chapter

24. GOAL FOR SHRINKAGE REDUCTION 193
   Kinds of merchandise shoplifted; shoplifting arrests by month; time of the day shoplifters were arrested; study of women's clothing shoplifted by women; all may help in a program of shrinkage reduction.

25. TRAINING SUPERVISORS IN STORE PROTECTION 198
   The key to shrinkage prevention or reduction rests with supervisors and management; All employes should be trained to minimize losses; Advice to supervisors, to make them aware of the problems, in order to perform the continuous training of all persons supervised.

26. REWARDS AND TRAINING EMPLOYES FOR PROTECTION 207
   Rewards often induce information of suspicions; All employes should be trained in any action to be taken to prevent thefts or cause legitimate arrests; Study of persons arrested on tips from employes, 211.

27. HOW STORE DETECTIVES SPOT SHOPLIFTERS 212
   A help for training both supervisors and store personnel.

28. HOW SOME EMPLOYES HAVE SPOTTED THIEVES 220
   Many employes possess the ability to prevent loss or help in the apprehension of thieves; Experiences which can help in employe training.

29. SUGGESTED BROCHURES AND REPORTS 226
   Rules, regulations, methods of loss prevention; all can be presented to employes in numerous ways; A few suggestions.

30. INTERNAL CONTROL 237
   Brief comments on Internal Control; Many books on accounting deal with the subject.

31. SHRINKAGE PREVENTION—SUMMARY 241
   The answer to shrinkage reduction exists in a planned, coordinated, program for personnel in all divisions.

32. MATERIAL FOR FURTHER STUDY OF PROTECTION 247
   Other publications can be helpful to the student of shrinkage prevention for stores; Those mentioned include many of the specific problems often encountered.

SHOPLIFTING AND SHRINKAGE PROTECTION FOR STORES

Chapter 1
RETAIL ACCOUNTING AND SHRINKAGE

INVENTORY or stock shortage, referred to as shrinkage, is loss due to unknown causes. Shrinkage is a factor of the retail method of book inventory, or selling price accounting, currently in use by most stores.

Ample material is available for anyone wishing to study retail accounting methods; however, a very brief reference must be made here because the final results of shrinkage are due in great measure to the effectiveness of protection.

Under the retail method of accounting, merchandise is received, transferred, sold, and inventoried on a retail price basis. In order to control the records, price changes, discounts, damages, and known losses must be reported accurately.

Shrinkage is an unknown quantity until the final physical inventory has been taken, tabulated, and consolidated with the accounting records. It is the difference between the sum of the closing inventory plus net sales, discounts, price changes, markdowns, and the starting inventory plus purchases.

The ultimate results, profit or loss, may be largely influenced by a satisfactory shrinkage figure. Shrinkage reduces both gross and net profit. A diminishing shrinkage can produce net profit results equal to increased sales.

In writing the following chapters, my aim has been to present ideas for merchants to reduce loss and shrinkage.

Chapter 2
HISTORY OF SHOPLIFTING

THE HISTORY of crime shows that professional shoplifting is an ancient, if not honorable, art, and the techniques of operation seem to have changed relatively little through the centuries. One of the earliest known accounts of shoplifting, written in 1597, describes "The Discovery of the Lifting Law," and the "lift," or shoplifter. Even then, there were diverse kinds of lifts; the common and rascal sort of lift, having a fine and nimble agility of the hand, and the gentlemen lifts. In describing a professional troupe, consisting of a "clout" and two "covers," only the language, but not the techniques of operation, differentiates this from a modern description.

> The higher degrees and gentlemen-lifts have to the performance of their faculty three parties of necessity, the lift, the marker, and the santar. The lift, attired in the form of a civil country gentleman, comes with the marker into some mercer's shop, haberdasher's, goldsmith's, or any such place where any particular parcels of worth are to be conveyed, and there he calls to see a bolt of satin, velvet, or any such commodity, and, not liking the pile, colour, or brack, he calls for more, and whilst he begins to resolve which of them most fitly may be lifted, and what garbage (for so he calls the goods stolen) may be most easily conveyed. Then he calls to the mercer's man and says, "Sirrah, reach me that piece of velvet or satin, or that jewel, chain, or piece of plate"; and whilst the fellow turns his back, he commits his garbage to the marker; for note the lift is without his cloak, in his doublet and hose, to avoid the more suspicion. The marker, which is the receiver of the lift's luggage, gives a wink to the santar, that walks before the window, and then, the santor going by in great haste, the marker calls to him and says, "Sir a word with you. I have a message to do unto you from a friend of yours, and the errand is of some importance."

"Truly, sir," says the santar, "I have very urgent business in hand, and as at this time I cannot stay. * * *"

"But one word, and no more," says the marker. And then he delivers him whatsoever the lift hath conveyed unto him; and then the santar goes on his way, who never came within the shop, and is a man unknown to them all.[1]

These lifts had their special receivers of their stolen goods.

Thus are these brokers and bawds, as it were, efficient causes of the lifter's villany, for, were it not their alluring speeches and their secret consellings, the lift for want of receivers should be fain to take a new course of life, or else be continually driven into great extremes for selling his garbage.[2]

One hundred years later (1726) the techniques of theft and the kinds of merchandise taken were similar, but the problem of the professional shoplifter had apparently become more acute to merchants. In *The Lives of Remarkable Criminals* is described a "troupe" consisting of Jane Holmes, "the woman Burton," and Mary Robinson. The three "fenced" their merchandise through the notorious "thief taker" Jonathan Wild. They were apprehended in the best modern manner.

In the summer of the year 1726, shoplifters became so common and so detrimental to the shopkeepers, that they made application to the Government for assistance in apprehending the offenders; and in order thereto, offered a reward and a pardon for any who would discover their associates in such practice.[3]

A stool pigeon, "the woman Burton," responded to the offer and informed on her associates, Jane Holmes and Mary Robinson, and their fence, Jonathan Wild. The three were apprehended, tried, and executed for their crimes.

Jane Holmes, of a good family, came up to London from the country when she was 16 years of age. She married a "sharp" trader who subsequently left her. She then took up shoplifting and

---

[1] The text prepared with notes and introduction by Judges, A.V., B.A., Assistant in the Department of History at the London School of Economics, *The Elizabethan Underworld*, New York, E. P. Dutton and Company, 1930, p. 170.

[2] *Ibid.* p. 171.

[3] Hayward, Arthur L. (ed): *Lives of the Most Remarkable Criminals*, George Routledge & Sons, Ltd., 1920, p. 375.

apparently practiced it quite successfully for many years, although she denied some of the crimes attributed to her by Burton. She was arrested and found guilty of stealing:

> * * * some twenty yards of straw-ground brocaded silks value £10, on the first of June 1726; of stealing, in the shop of Mr. Mather Herbert, forty yards of pink-coloured mantua silk, value £10, on the first of May, in the same year; of stealing in company with Mary Robinson, a silver cup of the value of £5, the goods of Elizabeth Dobbenson, on the seventh January; of stealing, in company of Mary Robinson afore-said, eighty yards of cherry-coloured mantua silk value £5, the goods of Joseph Bourn and Mary Harper, on the twenty-fourth of December.[1]

She was executed at Tyburn. Of Mary Robinson, her companion, the author says:

> The indiscretions of youth are always to be pitied, and often excused even by those who suffer most from them; but when persons grown up to years of discretion continue to pursue with eagerness the most flagitious courses, and grow in wickedness as they grow in age, pity naturally forsakes us, and they appear in so execrable a light that instead of having compassion for their misfortune we congratulate our country on being rid of such mobsters, whom nothing could tame, nor the approach even of death in a natural way hinder them from anticipating it by drawing on a violent one through their crimes.
>
> I am drawn to this observation from the fate of the miserable woman of whom we are now speaking, what her parents were or what her education it is impossible to say, since she was shy of relating them herself; and being 70 years old at the time of her execution, there was nobody then living who could give an account of her. She was indicted for stealing a silver cup in company with Jane Holmes, the property of Joseph Bourn and Mary Harper. On these facts she was convicted as the rest were, in the evidence of Burton, who, as is usual in such cases, they represented as a woman worse than themselves, who had drawn many of them into the commission of which she now deposed against them.
>
> * * * * *
>
> Possibly my readers may wonder how such a large quantity of silks were conveyed away. I think therefore proper to inform

---
[1] *Ibid.*, p. 376.

them that evidence Burton said; they had a contrivance under the petticoats not unlike two large hooks, upon which they laid a whole roll of silk, and so conveyed it away at once, while one of the company amused the people of the shop in some manner or other until they got out of reach; and by this means they had

Fashion During Reign of Louis XV, 1715-'74. "They had a contrivance under the petticoats not unlike two large hooks, upon which they laid a whole roll of silk, and so conveyed it away at once, while one of the company amused the people of the shop. . . ."

for years carried on together their trade with great success and as much safety, until the losses of the tradesmen ran so high as to induce them to take the method aforementioned, and quickly produce a discovery, not only of the persons of the offenders, but of the place also where they deposited the goods.[5]

A History of the Lives and Robberies of the Most Notorious

[5] *Ibid.,* p. 376.

"kleptomaniac," noting that the word had a special meaning in regard to shoplifting.

> There are generally but two classes of shoplifters—the regular criminal professional and the kleptomaniac. The very poor classes seldom take a hand in it. Poverty is held by the world to be the badge of crime, and the poor slattern who enters a store is sure to be so carefully watched that larceny is next to impossible. The shoplifter is always a person of fair appeal and she generally has a comfortable home. If she be a professional she may be one of a criminal community and her home may be shared by some other engaged in equally evil ways. If she be a kleptomaniac—and in shoplifting the word has peculiar significance—she is possibly a woman whose life in other respects is exemplary. It does seem strange that a wife and mother whose home is an honest one, who attends religious services regularly, and who seems far removed from the world of crime, should be carried away by her admiration of some trinket or knicknack as to risk her home, honor, and everything to secure it. But the annals of metropolitan offenses are full of instances of just this kind. It is the sex's fondness for finery that nine times out of ten gets them into trouble.[8]

Describing professional shoplifters, Inspector Brynes wrote:

> Two or three shoplifters have been known to enter large cloth dry goods or ostrich feather establishments in the morning just before business opening time, and while a porter or clerk was sweeping out. On some pretext or another one of the rogues engages the single guardian of the store in conversation and invariably succeeds in luring the unsuspecting man to the rear of the place. This is the thieves' opportunity, and when the porter's or clerk's back is turned to them the shoplifter's confederates are busy. In a twinkling they conceal whatever goods they are able to capture in false pockets upon their person. Then the first man tells his dupe that he will call again, and leaves the store after his associates.[9]

Benjamin Eldridge and William B. Watts, writing also in the United States, noted in 1890 that "the regular or professional

---

[8] Byrnes, Thomas F.: *Professional Criminals of America*, New York, 1886, p. 31-32.

[9] *Ibid.*, p. 33.

'shoplifter' is to be distinguished from the amateurs who occasionally yield to temptation, as well as from the kleptomaniac."[10]

As a matter of fact the woman shoplifters probably outnumber the men and the reason is apparent in the better facility for concealment of stolen goods which a women's dress secures. Large bags for holding plunder of every description are sometimes artfully draped and fastened under the skirt of a dress or the back of a cloak. This is technically known as the shoplifter's "kick," and experience perfected an improvement in this device in the form of the "hoisting kick" or short overskirt covering an ordinary dress skirt so stitched that the lining and the skirt make a complete bag round the body from the waist to the heels. This bag was often packed full of articles, slipped into it through a slit concealed by the apron overskirt. One notorious shoplifter was caught not long ago in the act of stealing a cake of scented soap. Upon examination sixteen yards of silk, fifty yards of lace, two pairs of silk stockings, one silk and one lace handkerchief, and a scarf pin were extracted from her clothing.[11]

Referring to amateurs Messers. Eldridge and Watts wrote:

There are doubtless thousands of dabblers in shop-lifting in our country as in the countries of the old world—boys who slyly pocket an apple or a handful of candy or even a knife or a necktie when the shop-keeper's head is turned—and girls who pick up a handkerchief or a bottle of cheap perfumery from the heaps on a counter. The little pilferers would commonly shrink from any considerable theft and, probably, most of them learn to be more honest as they grow older. But these first slips on the crust of crime are demoralizing and dangerous and most of our veteran thieves can trace their downfall from such a start.[12]

"Notes on Bibliokleptomania," *Bulletin of The New York Public Library*,[13] states that "it is possible to divide book thieves into two broad categories, namely, criminals and bibliomaniacs." "His-

---

[10] Eldridge, Benjamin, Superintendent of Police, Watts, Wm. B., Chief Inspector of the Detective Bureau, of the City of Boston: *Our Rival the Rascal*, Boston, Pemberton Publishing Company, 1897, p. 29-30.
[11] *Ibid.*, p. 31.
[12] *Ibid.*, p. 27.
[13] Thompson, Lawrence S.: Notes on Bibliokleptomania, *Bulletin of The New York Public Library*, Astor, Lenox and Tilden Foundations, Volume 48, Number 9, September 1944.

tory is full of examples of book ghouls," and he gives extensive references to thefts of whole libraries of books and manuscripts. "The history of bibliokleptomania goes back to the beginnings of libraries in Western Europe, and undoubtedly it could be traced back even further through the history of Greek and Oriental libraries."

Reference is made to thefts as early as the year 627, when, "the curse gained in popularity as an effective measure against book thieves and continued to be used until the introduction of the printed book."

While Mr. Thompson's account of book thefts deals mainly with thefts from libraries and collectors, by librarians, theologians, and scholars, mention is also made of thefts from shop-keepers in the nineteenth century. ". . . A well-known book thief, Dr. R—— of Lyons, never stole entire volumes . . .;" and ". . . towards the middle of the nineteenth century he (Sir Edward Fitzgerald, born of an illustrious English family, . . .) was well known among Parisian **bouquinistes** as **l'Anglais.** They tolerated his minor depredations of their stock, but one day he overstepped the bounds of their patience when he appropriated a polyglot Bible. He was apprehended and sentenced to two years in the penitentiary."

Has the progress of the centuries produced any changes in the profession of shoplifting or altered the effects of their actions, for merchants? The primary change is that shoplifters are not executed for their crimes today. Many of the professionals still travel in groups, still conceal bolts of silk and other items under or in their clothing, and have an outlet through a fence. It is not uncommon for a member of the group to give information on a confederate, especially after some disagreement, and it is a fact that all of us know that today many professional shoplifters are arrested because the problem of the shoplifter, to merchants, becomes more acute.

Shoplifters, like other criminals, have a decided tendency, almost mechanical, to repeat an established pattern in their activities. This is often the cause of their downfall.

A brief understanding of the background procedures of shoplifting activities over five centuries, as related by these various

History of Shoplifting

authors, helps us to better understand the problems of the twentieth century.

During the first decade of this century, the incidence of shoplifting, and the age and sex of the persons committing thefts from one department store, were not greatly unlike the present. *Example*—over a short period between 1900 and 1910:

Sex	Age	Merchandise Recovered
Female	33	1 waist $2.75
Female	17	1 waist $12
2 Males	15	moving pictures and books
Male	14	baseball book
Male	16	baseball
2 Females	16	ribbons, veil, handkerchiefs
Female	21	pocketbook
Male	12	golf ball
Female	37	12 fancy buttons, bolt of trimming
Male	12	watch $2
Male	17	watch $2
Male	17	card case

The available records for the period of 1901 to 1910 varied from those of more recent years in that they indicated *a larger percentage of juveniles were apprehended.*

The newspaper account of the arrest of a sixteen-year-old girl, in 1909, for shoplifting a mink muff, scarf, and gloves, value $158.50 read:

"... she stole furs to outshine rivals—to keep up an appearance as good as that of her classmates...."

A letter from the mother of a twelve-year-old boy, in 1911, indicates that *the juvenile delinquency problem is not a product of the post World War era.* Three twelve-year-old boys had each stolen whistles:

"... I wish to thank you for the manner in which you handled their misdemeanor. These surprising lapses from the watchings of their homes, which our children are often guilty of, is a matter of great perplexity to parents. I feel sure that all these boys acted on an impulse not before appearing in their experience. Our children are never allowed to go downtown alone. My son began his errors by an act of disobedience, going directly from school, unknown to me...."

Signed _____

In 1910 apparently professional shoplifters were still operating in groups and alone. One woman was prosecuted for stealing a pair of shoes of a value of $1.75, and she was fined $100 and costs, because of her prior record.

An increase in the number of shoplifting arrests during the period from 1911 to 1920 was probably due in part to the formation of enlarged protection departments by stores.

The pattern was similar; juveniles, amateurs, and professionals. The merchandise: fur neck pieces and muffs, blouses, skirts, coats, millinery, mesh bags, books, toys, watches, soap, etc., but no costume jewelry, or cosmetics.

In 1918, an anonymous letter, signed "A Customer" read: "You are missing a lot of fur coats in the men's section." In the letter advice was given to send to a certain hotel early in the morning to get a one-arm boy who "steals plenty and he wears one of them now."

A newspaper article in a Chicago paper in 1918 reports the recovery of some $2,000 worth of stolen lingerie and other feminine fripperies from the apartment of two women. Of this, $1,007 worth was identified by representatives of a department store. Both of the women had previous police records. "They distinguished themselves when they escaped from the automobile in which the patrolman was taking them to the Harrison Street Station Annex."

After their escape, the *Daily Bulletin of the Department of Police* issued a notice to arrest these two well known shoplifters:

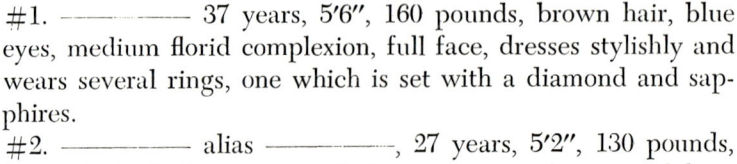

#1. ———— 37 years, 5'6", 160 pounds, brown hair, blue eyes, medium florid complexion, full face, dresses stylishly and wears several rings, one which is set with a diamond and sapphires.

#2. ———— alias ————, 27 years, 5'2", 130 pounds, brown hair, dark grey eyes, dark complexion, short round face, wears a cameo ring on a finger of each hand and a cameo brooch.

The two were again arrested with articles valued at $200 in their possession and charges of shoplifting were filed against them. Another newspaper article stated that #2 "was placed on probation some months ago when her attorney made the plea that an operation she had undergone caused her to become a kleptomaniac when she drank." He advanced the theory that alcohol caused "larceny germs."

A story from a Chicago newspaper of April 6, 1919:

LOVE OF BOOKS MAKES AGED MAN KLEPTOMANIAC.

No one paid any particular attention to the old man who walked into the book department.

Tall and spare, stooped shoulders, high forehead, thin gray locks curling over ears, pale face and aquiline nose—all bespoke intellect and breeding—the typical book-lover to be seen any day browsing among the stalls of second-hand book stores.

Passing with unconcealed disdain, the counter on which reposed the latest fiction, he paused beside a table laden with classics. . . .

He was arrested after stealing a set of Dickens. The report of a doctor from the psychopathic hospital, where he was examined, was that the man was a constitutional psychopathic inferior suffering from schizophrenia.

Despite this fact, however, he is extremely well educated and extremely intelligent. We may be able to cure him, but I am inclined to think he will need constant custodial care.

The man had claimed that strange voices told him to steal and that he was the victim of impulses which he could not resist! The not-unusual claim!!

The problems confronting retailers and stores protection personnel today are as varied and as rare as the preceding cases.

nished home in one of the suburbs, believed by the police to be a clearing house for a gang of shoplifters operating throughout the middle west.

Between $10,000 and $12,000 worth of furs and other valuable articles, believed to be stolen merchandise, was seized. I have never seen nor heard of the man since this case but I have had numerous experiences with the woman.

Her habit of fighting court convictions has helped to establish Illinois law. She was arrested in Rockford, Illinois, on April 14, 1936, and charged with the larceny of one woman's silk suit of the value of $19.75, and two pajama suits, each of the value of $10.95. She was found guilty by a jury.

Her attorneys appealed the case to the Supreme Court of Illinois, where judgement was affirmed.[3]

There was little dispute as to the facts in the case. While on the third floor of the store, she had picked up the merchandise, alleged to have been stolen by her, and walked down the stairs to the second floor and into the rest room on that floor. Later she deposited the merchandise on a table in the rest room.

One employe of the store had testified to having seen her coming down the stairway carrying her coat on her left arm and that she was tucking her coat in at the bottom.

Another witness testified that the woman came out of the rest room with her coat on; that she carried her hand across her abdomen, and the witness noted what she characterized as a "bunch" at that place, by reason of which the coat "stuck out"; that she approached the counter where the witness was standing, and upon being asked if she wanted something, made no reply but returned to the rest room. The witness followed her, but despite the fact that she stood on the stool of an adjoining toilet, was unable to see what the woman was doing. The woman came out of the toilet booth she had entered and sat down at a table. The witness walked away for a minute, and, on returning, saw the suit and two pajama suits lying on the table.

Another witness, an employe of the store, went into the rest room and saw the woman come out of one of the toilet booths,

[3] People v Baker, 365 Ill. 328 (1937).

walk to the table, and open her coat. The silk suit and two pajama suits fell from her coat onto the table.

One witness, a customer of the store, testified that she saw the woman take articles from one of the counters and put them under her coat.

Another employe of the store testified to having followed the woman from the store into an alley, and upon seeing a policeman cross the alley on a nearby street, whistled to attract his attention, whereby the woman ran down the alley in the opposite direction and disappeared. He later saw her in a restaurant where she was arrested.

During the trial, the state had proven the essential elements of larceny, which has been defined in Illinois as: ". . . the felonious stealing, taking, and carrying away the personal goods of another, by which the owner is deprived of possession and the thief acquires possession for an appreciable period of time, though such period may be for but a moment, and any change of location whereby control of the article is, with intent to steal, transferred from the owner to the thief is sufficient evidence of taking away."

In Illinois it is not necessary for a thief to leave the premises with stolen merchandise before an arrest can be made. It is only necessary to prove intent to steal.

For example:

> If one feloniously takes the goods of another from their accustomed place, although he is detected before they are actually carried away, the crime of larceny is complete, and where a shoplifter, after taking goods from a show case and putting them in his overcoat pocket, runs away, leaving his overcoat lying on another show case, the crime is larceny though his possession was brief and the goods were not removed from the store.[4]

The woman who had used the name of Baker, when arrested in Rockford, must have known this because of her previous contacts with the law, yet she fought her prison sentence by appealing the case to the Supreme Court of the State of Illinois. The funds to

[4] People v Lardner, 300 Ill. 264 (1921).

finance her appeal, no doubt, came from further shoplifting sorties, as I have never heard of her being employed.

Sometime after this woman had completed her penitentiary sentence, she was again arrested, this time for petit larceny. Our chinaware section had reported several losses of expensive plates from a shop-like room. Investigation revealed that the area could not be watched satisfactorily from the sales floor but an enclosed stairway was located adjacent to the room. By scraping some paint from the glass partition it was possible to watch the corner of the room from which the plates disappeared.

We were sure that the culprit would return. If an amateur collector had taken the plates, she was sure to return. Professionals follow the same pattern, that is, if successful in thefts from one store or one section in a store, **they will return and steal again. The only problem is a question of time.** One of our operators was an expert in working a "plant"; she was patience personified, but fortunately she did not have to wait long.

Baker, the woman of many aliases, was apprehended in the act of stealing, but this time it was only plate holders. True to form, she used a new name, claiming to be married again.

When her case came up in court her attorney asked for a jury trial, a procedure not too common in petit larceny cases. In April 1945, she was again the subject of newspaper articles. The headlines in one paper read "Shoplifter's Record Read in Municipal Court Test."

The article stated that the judge had announced he was breaking a Municipal Court precedent when he ordered the past record of a defendant read before the jury after it had reached a decision of guilty. "Faces of the jurors hardened noticeably as a clerk from the Bureau of Identification read the record of 22 arrests and 3 penitentiary terms for shoplifting against Mrs. ———."

The jurors had found her guilty of stealing four wooden plate holders worth about $4. After hearing her record, they rendered a decision setting the penalty at one year in the County Jail and a fine of $100.

The attorney had kept his client off the stand so that her record could not be questioned but the judge stated he realized it would be a test case. He did not believe a jury could give a just sentence if the record of a defendant were unknown to it. It was the first time a jury had been asked to defer decision on a penalty after reaching a verdict, but the judge said he took the step because "society should be protected."

This time she received value for the cost of her attorney filing an appeal. The case was sent back to the Municipal Court for a new trial and her attorney agreed to plead her guilty on a bench trial. She was sentenced to 90 days in the County Jail.

The record of 22 arrests for shoplifting has been increased by additional arrests both in and out of Chicago. But apparently she thought that she could do better as a pickpocket than a shoplifter.

A newspaper headline in November 1954 read, "Woman Grabs Arm of Law." Mrs. ——— stuck her hand in the wrong bag. The victim was a new store detective, in training, and her trainer was in a perfect spot to see the attempt to rob. Twenty months passed and the case had not been disposed of in the courts. As is customary in many cases, several continuances were given her attorney, for "professional reasons." We consider that such delays meant that he had not yet been paid for his services! Then a statement from a doctor saying that she was unable to appear because of a physical condition was the excuse for further continuances. Merchants, the public, and the tax payers would benefit if her health condtion would keep her home, but it was reported that she had been seen in suburban stores about the time she was too ill to appear in court.

It is almost a certainty that merchants will be victimized by her as long as she lives.

In 1951, Illinois House Bill 1187 was passed and signed by the Governor. This new statute amended the Criminal Code and provides that any person who has been convicted three times for larceny, in any degree, and who subsequently commits a petty larceny of goods, may be punished as a habitual criminal and imprisoned in the State Penitentiary for not less than one year and not more than five years.

The $4 plate holder case was prior to the passage of this law; however, we have used it successfully in prosecutions since its passage.

We were the first in Cook County to use the law. A man who

had worked for our store, before we knew him to be a thief, repeatedly shoplifted merchandise under $50 valuation, the current dividing point between petit and grand larceny in Illinois. The value had been raised from $15 to $50 some years before. The last time we arrested him he was sentenced on a habitual, in addition to a petit larceny charge.

A local newspaper story in May 1948 may explain his reasons for confining his thefts to less than $50. It was headlined, "This tale of love has a 'lift' to it. If it weren't for a woman, I wouldn't be in trouble; guess I'm just chivalrous." The humorous story explained the interview of the police captain with this man who was to appear in court on a narcotics complaint while his girl friend was to answer to a petty larceny charge. They explained to the captain that they had to stick to the small stuff because, "we don't want to go to the penitentiary. Now in New York anything less than $100 is petty larceny. There a pair of smart boosters can make enough in a day to live like human beings." The girl cut in with, "Just the same, I want to be near my mother who lives here when my baby comes along in September or October."

In another case the Supreme Court of the State of Illinois held that it is not error to charge defendant in his proper name as well as under an alias in an indictment.

> In prosecution for larceny, testimony of special police officers that they had known defendants under other names was admissible for purpose of identification and substantiation of charge in indictment that defendants were known under aliases charged therein. Admission of such evidence was not reversible error on ground that such evidence suggested previous criminal records.[5]

Professional shoplifters are most always agreeable upon arrest and will usually appear to cooperate with store personnel. Probably the reason that they identify themselves with an alias is the hope that they will not be recognized. The store detective who can identify these professionals, and identify them by name, is an asset to his organization.

On June 15, 1940, two women were arrested for shoplifting one

[5] People v Jedynak et al. 377 Ill. 621 (1941).

purse and two straw hats. I had previously helped to prosecute one of them along with a male companion, for stealing bolts of silk, which she concealed under her coat.

When called as a witness on behalf of the People, the store detective testified that she had seen the defendants at the purse counter. She had known one of them for about six years. She saw these women handle the purses and observed one of the defendants select a white purse and hand it to the other one, who then stepped back and placed it under her coat. They then left the store and the detective followed them and saw the one take the purse from under her coat and place it in a paper bag. The defendants proceeded to the men's store, located in another building, and the detective called the office of the company for assistance.

Another special officer joined the witness and together they observed the one defendant hand two hats to the other one, who again stepped in back and placed the hats under her coat. They proceeded to the vestibule where the hats were placed in a bag.

In this case the defendants took the stand and denied having taken the property. The one defendant testified that she ran a beauty parlor and that the pocketbook was given to her by a Mrs. Smith shortly after Christmas, and that Mrs. Smith had gone to California on a vacation and she did not know whether she was still there or not. She made no effort to find her, nor did she remember Mrs. Smith's first name. Neither charged that there was any intimidation or threats or promises of immunity made to them at any time while under arrest.

A guilty verdict was returned by the jury and then the defendants claimed error on two points: first, that testimony of the confession was inadmissible, and, second, that it was error to permit the witness to testify that she had known the one defendant under another name prior to the date upon which she was arrested.

The police officer who was called in on the arrest also testified that he knew this defendant by two other names.

Judgment of the jury was affirmed. It was held that testimony regarding a confession was admissible and that it is not error to charge a defendant in his proper name as well as under an alias in an indictment. The challenged testimony was admissible.

In November 1948 a man was arrested for the theft of a pair of gloves. The gloves were inexpensive and there was a possibility that he might not have been prosecuted, except for the fact that he carried a kit of tools in his brief case. Apparently it was a burglar's kit, used to pick locks. The man was dapper and congenial, but a check of the Bureau of Identification files revealed news for the reporters.

The headlines of an article in one paper were: "$2.95 Gloves Theft May Return Parolee to Prison for Life." This shoplifter's record goes back to 1914 in Lima, Ohio. His last previous sentence, in September 1935, was to Attica (New York) prison for 15 years to life for burglary. He was paroled for life in August 1945. The theft of the gloves, a violation of parole, could return him to prison. He had served terms in the Ionia, Michigan, Mansfield, Ohio, and Michigan City, Indiana, prisons. He was a cellmate of Dillinger in the Michigan City prison.

Another article related the conversation of the Deputy Chief of Detectives, at a police show up, who asked if they were acquainted. "Sure," the prisoner replied, "I was the guy picked up in 1934 for harboring Dillinger."

The criminals with whom store detectives must match wits are usually not vicious and are often clever. It requires finesse to apprehend them, and interrogation must bring out all pertinent facts. Bits of information must be pieced together and catalogued for future use and it is extremely important to know when to use it.

One of the first experiences I had with a clever professional shoplifter, whose activities in one way or another I have followed all through twenty-two years, developed by chance. I had been given information that "hot" merchandise was being sold from a certain home. A short time later one of our detectives brought two attractive women into the office. They had stolen the type of merchandise which had been described and I cannot now recall just what it was in our conversation that caused me to associate them with my information.

I remember that they were both reluctant to give any information about themselves and flatly refused to tell where they lived. I said, "You are ——— and live at ———." One of the two (it later developed that they were sisters) collapsed and fell on the floor in a faint. One admitted that I was correct, but refused permission to search the home. They were hurried to the detective bureau and a search warrant was obtained from the court.

The one woman accompanied detectives and myself to her home where we found a merchandise display room. It had been fitted with hanging rods which were filled with merchandise.

This woman has been arrested at different times since then with a number of known shoplifters and she became so well known that she was readily spotted. Therefore, she trained other young women to work for her. Her husband had two court cases pending and when we arrested him recently, with a young woman companion, he stated that he and his wife were separated and that she was seriously ill with tuberculosis but that she was well off financially.

How do these shoplifters become financially independent? This one has always driven expensive cars and has owned beautiful homes which she has changed from time to time when the police learned of her whereabouts and became too inquisitive. At one time she had a so-called legitimate business, a candy store.

Then came a news story, headlined, "7 Nabbed in Theft Ring After 5-day Watch." According to the report, police had kept a patient vigil of the candy store after a man reported he purchased a $175 electric drill there for $40. A check of the serial number of the drill showed it to be loot of a Thanksgiving day burglary of a manufacturing company.

Among the seven arrested were three clerks of her candy store; one of them was a nephew of another recognized "fence" in Chicago and had applied to me, at one time, for a position as a store detective; another one had been arrested by us for shoplifting. He also helped to establish Illinois law by appealing a sentence imposed in Winnebago County.[6]

He and two companions were indicted jointly on two counts; the first charged them jointly with stealing two men's suits; the second count charged each with stealing the same property and also charged each with having theretofore been convicted of a

[6] People v Tabet, 402 Ill. 93 (1949).

felony, for which he was sentenced. Motions for new trial and an arrest of judgment were overruled, and the defendants were sentenced to the penitentiary.

The principal errors complained of were that the defendants were unlawfully arrested without a warrant and that the evidence should have been suppressed because of unlawful search of an automobile and seizure of articles found therein.

The three men entered a clothing store in Rockford and two of them approached a lady clerk and asked for size 34 moleskin breeches. The clerk inquired of the owner of the store, who had never heard of that type of breeches, and as he started forward to see the customers, he noticed that the third man put two suits under his top coat and started out the door. The other two men blocked his way and he had to cut over to another aisle to get through. He called, saying, "I am going to wait on you," but the thief got outside, and when the owner reached the door, was nowhere to be seen. The other two men denied being with the thief.

An exchange of information was made with other clothing stores and the alertness of a salesman in one resulted in the police arresting the three men. No warrant had been issued for the arrest of any of the three but they were arrested on suspicion.

When arrested, Tabet had a set of keys and a license for a 1941 Dodge. Search for that car was ordered giving the license number and soon thereafter a car bearing those plates was located, but it was a 1946 Chrysler. The officers found clothing on the back seat of the car and in the trunk they found three suit cases, three suits, and other clothing. Two of the suits found were identified as being those taken from the one store visited. The officers had no search warrant when they searched Tabet, nor when they entered the car and the trunk.

There was no error by the officers making the arrest. Illinois law has established that an officer has a right to arrest without a warrant where he has reasonable grounds to believe that the person arrested is guilty of a crime where, in fact, a crime has been committed.

It was the opinion of the Supreme Court that the arrest without a warrant in this case was justified and proper. It has been held that where the arrest without a warrant is justified the accompanying search of the person is also justified, and that where one is legally arrested for an offense, what is found on his person, or in his control, which it is unlawful for him to have, and which may be used to prove the offense, may be seized and held as evidence in the prosecution. Judgment of the lower court was affirmed.

Another one of the seven persons seized at the candy store was the wife of a man who was also arrested when he appeared with two shopping bags filled with clothing bearing labels of various department stores.

Another shoplifter, who had been arrested with the candy store owner several times, owned a tavern in an adjoining store. A policeman, assigned to the district station, recently informed me that both shops were closed, that the two women had suffered some disagreement and threw bricks through each other's show windows.

It is not unusual for professional thieves to have personal disagreements:

> Six women "worked"—with great success—. A split occurred because two of the women became on familiar terms with the husbands of two of their accomplices. The police immediately received anonymous letters with the result that all save two of the gang were arrested.[7]

Professional shoplifters will try to buy their way free. The People's testimony in the Tabet-Rockford case shows that the defendants had offered to "make it right with them" (the police) if they would reduce the charge to petty larceny. The owner of the tavern also tried to buy her way out at one time.

One of our detectives had just returned from Naval Service in Okinawa, and like other service men, he was finding it somewhat difficult to settle to civilian ways. He came to my office one day and handed me a $50 bill with the explanation that he didn't know why he had stopped two women, and when one offered him the money, he took it and walked away.

Our special police are all trained to make an arrest only after they have seen a theft committed. This detective was standing

[7] Bishop, Cecil: *Women and Crime*, London, Chatto and Windus. 1931.

near an exit, probably dreaming of the Pacific, when a saleswoman came to him and said, "stop those two women." He followed them to the street, stopped them, and immediately realized he did not know what they had done. So when the one, later identified as the tavern owner, offered him $50 to be released, he took it.

What should we do? It has always been my policy that all our protection personnel remain independent of criminals. I think that has been part of our success. The only thing that I could do was to make a record of the serial number of the bill, seal it up and place it in the safe. I then instructed the operator to bring the woman to the office the next time he saw her.

About five months passed and early one afternoon the operator phoned and told me the woman who had given him the $50 bill was on the fifth floor, with another woman, not the one she was with the day he stopped her. I told him to bring the one to the office.

I recognized her immediately, informed her that I was not going to have her locked up this time, but that I had another matter to discuss with her. I got the $50 from the safe, took a receipt from her, warned her to never again try to pay off any of my operators, and put her on notice that she was to stay out of our properties, and that she would be a trespasser at any time she was found in the store. Then I escorted her from the building.

Her companion apparently had phoned her attorney, because about three hours later he phoned, wanting to know what I was doing with his client. He had gone to the police station to make bond for her and she had not yet arrived. He could not understand why I had not locked her up, but I did not explain. Instead I told him to talk to his client. The next time I met the attorney in court he made it a point to talk to me. He said, "I have never heard anything like that. You know, my clients don't like you and I have told them to stay away from your store because I won't defend them if they are caught there." I told him that the "dislike" was mutual.

I believe that he did tell his clients to keep away from me. We did not see nor arrest any of them for many months.

The last time we did arrest the ex-tavern owner was recently when she was in the store with another well known shoplifter.

Both had previously been put on notice to stay out, so we picked them up, had a number of our salespeople look at them, and locked them up on a trespass charge.

A family tree type of a chart, showing all the contacts I have had with shoplifters who have been associated with the candy store owner, whose sister fell from a chair in a faint, would be quite extensive. An examination of her income tax reports would be most interesting, because I classify her as a true professional.

Another professional shoplifter, whom I have known for years, usually works alone. She has raised a family and financed her children through private schools and universities on her gains. She has assured me that her children are not in the racket and the last time we arrested her, she informed me that her youngest son had graduated from the university and was now in the armed services.

Some of the trade papers and magazines have stated that professional shoplifters are operating more and more in suburban area stores and less in downtown stores, principally because protection coverage outside the cities is only a fraction of that in the big downtown stores.[8]

It is a fact that the professionals also tour the smaller towns throughout the country. We are always interested in the conviction of a professional in the smaller cities because it seems that penitentiary sentences are secured more frequently.

One professional that we had arrested several times, and known by numerous aliases, was arrested in the city of Joliet in December, 1952. On January 9, 1953, the grand jury of Will County returned an indictment charging her with the crime of larceny of two suits. She petitioned for a change of venue to a county other than Will. There was an order denying the change of venue, and there was a jury trial. The jury returned a verdict finding the defendant guilty, motion for a new trial was overruled and the defendant was sentenced to a minimum term of nine years and a maximum of ten years.

The points relied upon for reversal were that the People failed to prove that the ownership of the property alleged to have been stolen was in the corporation, as charged in the indictment.

[8] *Women's Wear Daily*, June 29, 1953.

Argument:

"It is our contention that upon objection to oral testimony of proof of corporate franchise, it was necessary for the prosecution to prove the existence of the corporation by introduction of the charter of the corporation or a certified copy thereof, or by proving user."[9]

Proof of corporate existence may be shown by oral testimony when not objected to. The Supreme Court of Illinois affirmed the judgment, stating the corporate existence of the alleged owner and the ownership of the stolen property was abundantly established.

Certified copies of corporate existence can be secured from the Secretary of State. It is advisable for detectives to take one of these copies to court. Most times corporate existence is not challenged but we have had cases where the defense attorney will ask for proof.

Retailers will suffer shrinkage as long as professionalism exists in shoplifting. The criminal records of arrests are proof that the professional travels extensively. Retailers in smaller communities suffer and inquire of protection personnel in larger stores for methods to combat their losses.

Professional shoplifters from New York, Detroit, St. Louis, Kansas City, and many other localities have been arrested shoplifting in Chicago. The local professionals have been arrested in many other cities, often in the smaller ones within a day's drive from home.

At one time a questionnaire, or notice, was issued by the Retail Dry Goods Association, "Organized Thefts of Clothing."

"Will you please let us know whether you are losing much apparel merchandise? There is considerable evidence which indicates that gangs are at work stealing better class men's clothing from retail stores. We understand that frequently two men and a woman work together. While one man is being fitted with the woman criticising, the other man, left to himself, slips up to the better clothing cases and selects a high priced suit which he manages to conceal under his vest and coat by an ingenious arrangement of hooks. He clears out and there is

[9] People v Gordon, 5 Ill. 2nd 91 (1955).

another high priced suit missing from that department.

Apparently this traffic is well organized. The thieves are said to ship their loot to various clearing houses maintained for that purpose where the goods are sold to certain retailers who are not too curious about where the goods came from."

Two females, fur coat shoplifters, were reported in custody in Wisconsin. They were arrested after attempting to shoplift two expensive fur coats in a Madison store. "It is believed that these women have been operating extensively in the midwest." They are both well known to Chicago store detectives. The criminal record of one of them dates from 1918, and in addition to arrests in Chicago and Madison, she had been arrested in New Orleans, St. Louis, Youngstown, Ohio, and Washington, D.C. Some of the arrests and convictions were for violation of Federal Narcotic Laws.

THE FOLLOWING IS A SUMMARY OF THE SHOPLIFTERS' METHOD OF OPERATION

The two women apprehended in this case apparently made a day's trip out of Chicago with the intent of returning to their homes the same day. They would go to a furrier shop or a department store, merchandising quality furs, where the tallest of the two women, would attract the attention of the clerks in an attempt to keep them from her partner, while she would take a fur piece from a rack and place it underneath her skirt.

The skirt worn by the booster contained between ten and fifteen yards of material with an elastic waist. She would place the fur piece into the skirt from the top and hook it upon large blanket type safety pins that had been attached to her undergarments.

The conversation of the first woman with the clerks would be to the effect that they were waiting for her daughter to help them pick out a coat for her. The daughter generally was supposed to have been in a day or two previously and looked up the coats.

The subjects usually parked their car on a side street about two or three blocks away from the store that they entered. Both women are very intelligent. They have completed University educations.[10]

[10] *Wisconsin Law Enforcement Bulletin*, Volume IV, No. 3.

The State Crime Laboratory made an examination of the debris taken from their car by the "Vacuum Sweeper Technique." Animal hairs were identified as dyed mink, natural mink, dyed persian lamb, and dyed squirrel.

Professional shoplifters do not confine their activities to fur shops and clothing stores. The woman who was arrested for stealing two suits, from the Joliet store, had also been arrested, along with a male companion, for the theft of diamond jewelry from a shop in Miami, Florida. Antique shops, sporting goods and hardware stores, have been victimized. Supermarkets frequently suffer the loss of canned hams, cartons of cigarettes and cans of coffee.

The professional thief may steal from some store, every day of the year. He usually selects higher priced merchandise and may steal in quantity. He is generally most skilled and experienced in methods of stealing and is difficult to apprehend. If not detected or deterred he can cause great shrinkage for stores.

Chapter 4
PREVAILING SHOPLIFTING METHODS

A SHOPLIFTER is one guilty of shoplifting from a store or shop, during business hours. In the jargon of the underworld, shoplifting is referred to as boosting and the shoplifter as a booster. It may be helpful in understanding shoplifting methods to know some of the slang of thieves which has come into common usage among police and protection personnel.

Any booster at work may bob, boost, jam, clout, jam-snatch, lift, nab, nick, bag, annex, collar, collect, cop, grab off, palm, pick, pinch, pull, score, snag, swipe, any one of which means to steal.

Boosting under the protection of an overcoat could be called benny-work. Occasionally a booster will clout and lam, meaning to steal and run.

A pennyweighter or stone getter is a jewel thief, but a hard rock boy or ice man is strictly a diamond thief. A skin worker is a fur thief, and a worm worker a silk thief.

Professional shoplifters often wear and use booster pants or bloomers. The arrangement is usually a pair of bloomers with elastic bands at the knees and around the waist. The waist may be fastened to a skirt waist band, or it may be unattached, but the skirt also has an elastic belt. The skirt and bloomers can be pulled away from the body and articles quickly dropped in, while being shielded with an open coat, benny-work fashion.

There are variations of the booster bloomers. One old time professional wore a dress with a knee length peplum, or over-skirt. When she lifted the over-skirt, there was a V shaped cut out of the under-skirt, which allowed her to slip merchandise into her bloomers, under cover of the peplum.

An example of a professional booster working with bloomers, made news in 1953. "Bloomer Girl Lines 2 Pairs in Costly Furs." The woman of many aliases, and a record of shoplifting dating from 1922, in all parts of the country, was arrested on the com-

Variation of booster bloomers. Instead of a blouse and skirt with elastic waist band, one professional booster wore a dress with over-skirt, which allowed her to slip merchandise into her bloomers, under cover of it.

plaint of a furrier, whose shop was located on the 10th floor of a State Street building. Her last previous arrest in Chicago had been in 1930.

Upon examining her at the police station, the matron found that she was wearing two pairs of bloomers. Inside the bloomers were a mink coat, valued at $4,000, and a mink cape $800. She had slipped into a fur vault to get the garments, as they were not displayed on the selling floor.

A substitute for bloomers is a cloth sack or bag arrangement it and slip both from the counter, or place the article between the pages of the paper or magazine.

A salesperson in the handkerchief section became suspicious of a woman and called protection. While the woman handled handkerchiefs she had a newspaper lying on the counter. She would place the handkerchiefs she was stealing between the folds of the newspaper and after she left she removed them and placed them in her purse.

A woman looking at watches was holding a newspaper close to her left side. It was held in an odd manner and suddenly she transferred a watch from her right to her left hand. While looking at other watches in her right hand, she slipped the watch from her left hand into a side pocket of her dress. The newspaper was held in a position to hide the pocket.

Fitting rooms are a hazard for clothing departments. Thieves will steal garments that the salesperson takes in, or sometimes will carry them in themselves. They may be worn out under other clothing; an old garment may be left and the new one worn out; or they may be concealed in a bag, package, or wrapped in a coat and carried out.

At one time two young men were suspected of stealing slacks, but the operator did not know exactly how they were carried out. A week later when the same two men entered the sportswear department the operator was there to observe their actions. Each one of the men selected a pair of slacks which they rolled up and then covered with another pair thrown over the arm. They both carried the slacks into a fitting room.

They put on the slacks that were carried openly and came out to be fitted, but the fitter informed them that the garments were too large to be cut down satisfactorily. They stated that those were the slacks they wanted and that they would look further.

While the men were on the selling floor talking to the fitter, the operator had found the rolled up slacks concealed in the legs of their own pants. When the men returned to the fitting room, each one wrapped a pair of $44 slacks tightly around his waist, put his own trousers on and fastened his belt, then walked out.

Unprotected fitting rooms have been used for wholesale thefts. Regardless of the season, checkers at fitting rooms are an asset.

42   *Shoplifting and Shrinkage Protection*

A young man, carrying two booster boxes, was apprehended stealing phonograph records. Both boxes were wrapped, tied, and addressed, so they appeared to be ready for mailing. One box had a hinged slit at one end so

Prevailing Shoplifting Methods

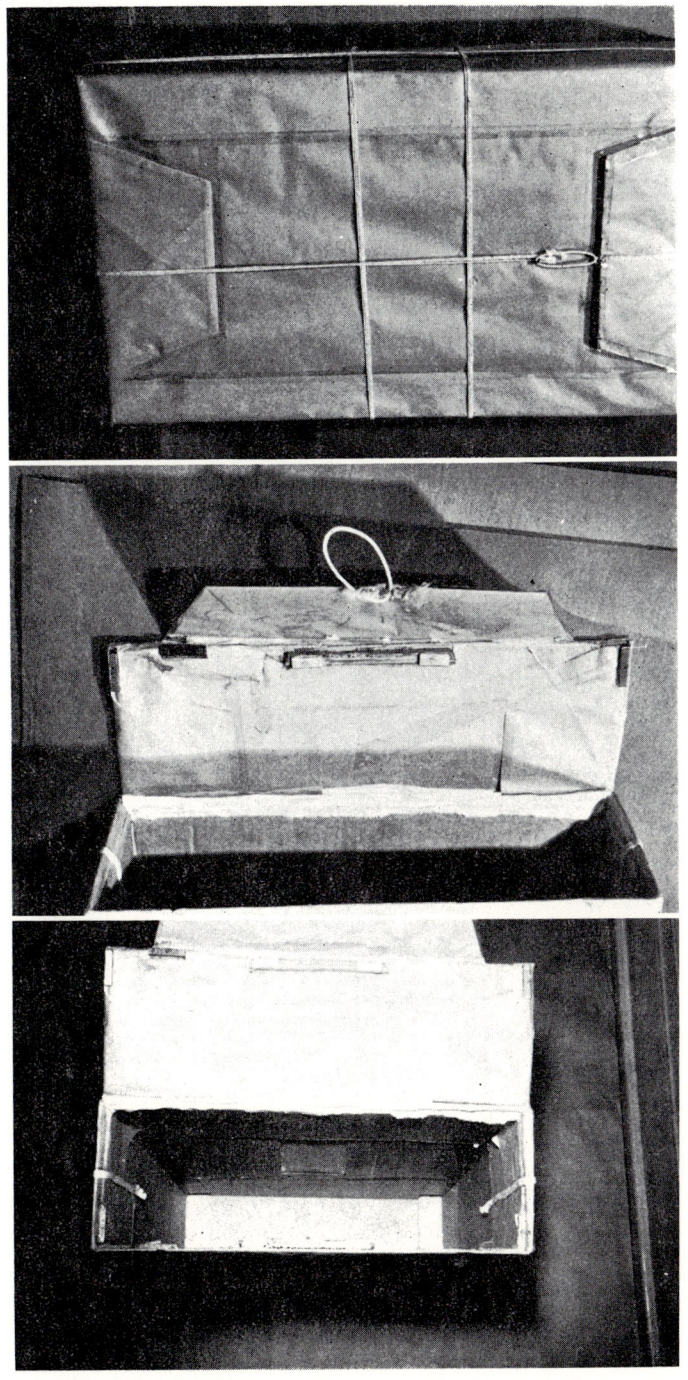

that records could be easily inserted. The other box, hinged at one end, had a loop that caught over a metal hook to hold it in place.

44   *Shoplifting and Shrinkage Protection*

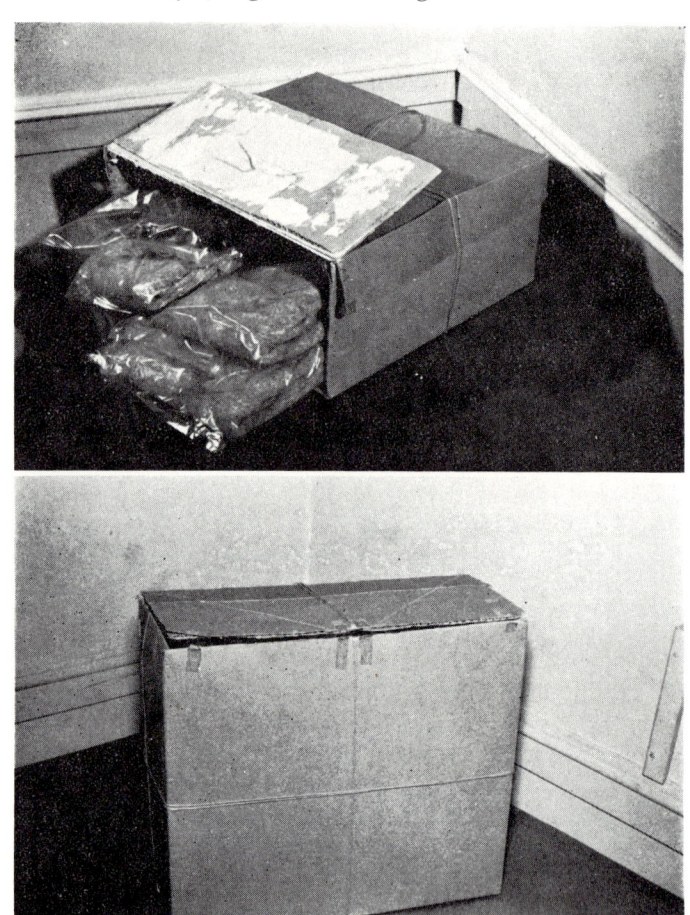

Another booster box, crudely constructed, was also hinged at the top so merchandise could be easily inserted. When closed it also looked like a tied box.

At one time while experimenting without checkers, reports of thefts were received from women's ready-to-wear sections throughout the store. Buyers or their assistants would notify protection of the loss of the best and most exclusive garments. In several instances a woman without coat and hat had been questioned regarding merchandise she carried into a fitting room. She would state that she was a part time employe working in the section for the day, but later the garments were discovered missing.

A further check of the records of salespeople assigned to the department for the day left the woman unaccounted for.

When the woman was arrested she had $900 worth of coats and suits in her possession and in public lockers in neighboring stores.

She would leave her coat and hat in a fitting room, pose as a saleswoman, and select the best garments on the floor, take them to the fitting room where she would package them, replace her coat and hat and leave the store.

Public lockers in a store must be a calculated risk. They are used by boosters but so are checkrooms that are available for public use. Protection personnel can spot suspects at lockers. It is advisable to watch, periodically, public lockers and checkrooms in neighboring drug stores and transportation stations. Both shoplifters and employes may be discovered and followed. Many arrests are made of persons first spotted at lockers.

In downtown areas where no parking facilities are available immediately adjacent to a store, a booster will sometimes have an accomplice driving a car around the block.

Suit cases, traveling bags, and brief cases are used to hold stolen merchandise. In fact all types of carrying cases have been used. One man was arrested twice for stealing a quantity of merchandise and carrying it away in a viola case which he carried.

As an operator passed the woman's glove counter, she noticed a man with a zipper bag that was un-zipped. He seemed to be selecting gloves and then he looked around quickly, folded six pairs of gloves, and dropped them into the bag and walked to the exit.

Methods of shoplifting are as varied as the ingenuity of man, but the most common aid is a shopping bag or just a plain paper bag.

A survey of several hundred consecutive arrests showed that 12.6 per cent of the shoplifters used shopping bags, and 20 per cent used paper bags.

Shopping bags carried by boosters are of brown paper, bags with store names, cloth, plastic, knitting bags, in fact any kind of an open top bag that articles can be quickly dropped into.

How some of the shopping bags were used and the reasons the lifters attracted attention:

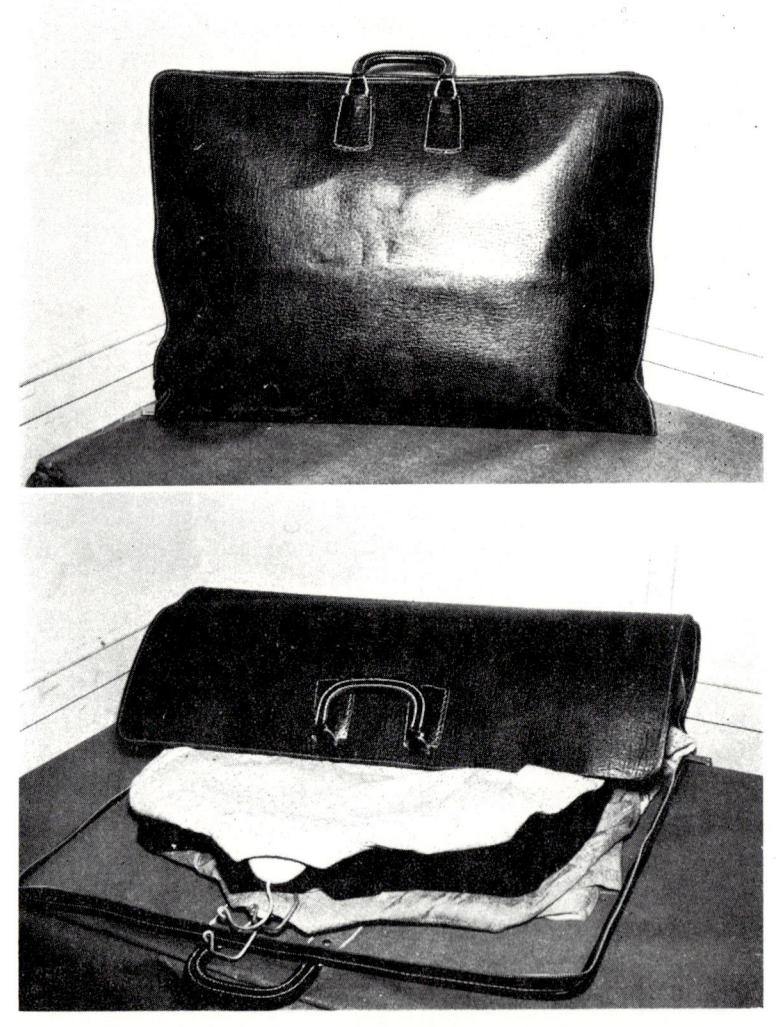

All types of carrying cases have been used. One man was apprehended with three men's suits in this one.

One young woman was observed to be watching over the top of a dress rack while she handled dresses. She removed one from a hanger, without looking at the dress, folded it and put it in a shopping bag which was at her feet on the floor. She went to a washroom and into a booth where she removed the price tag, then returned to the dress section where she took another dress the same way.

Two boys 16 and 18 years of age, each carrying paper shopping bags were watched. After looking around at the salespeople, each put a shirt into his bag. Each took several articles from other sections.

A girl who had no packages but bought a shopping bag was followed. She went to a counter, picked up a wallet and dropped it into the bag, then went to the book section where she took two books and placed them in the bag.

As a young woman walked down an aisle she took a folded shopping bag from under her arm, opened it, then went to a dress section. She removed a dress from a rack and concealed it under her jacket, then left the section. After leaving the section she put the dress in the shopping bag.

Men rarely carry shopping bags, so when a well dressed young man stopped at the greeting card counter, carrying one, he was watched. He stole one greeting card, then proceeded to take a number of phonograph records.

The way a woman held a shopping bag with the open end near the top of a counter was the reason she was watched. She carried a handkerchief in the other hand which she placed over a wallet and slipped it from the counter into the bag. She went to another section, looked at paper weights, then placed the handkerchief over an ash tray, walked to a corner and dropped it into the bag.

A woman wearing dark glasses, as she carried four dresses into a fitting room, drew attention. In a few minutes she came out with only two dresses and the fitting room was empty. She was followed to a washroom on another floor and there she removed a folded shopping bag from her purse, went into a toilet booth, removed the two dresses from her bloomers and placed them in the bag.

A small boy stole overalls and a belt and concealed them in his shopping bag. Two little girls took skirts. Three little boys made a game of helping themselves to toy automobiles. One had

While in a toilet booth, an operator heard paper being rattled in the adjoining booth but the toilet was not flushed. When a woman came out she carried a paper bag that appeared to be overloaded or more bulky than a normal purchase. She went to a dress section, removed a dress from a hanger, twirled it into a ball which she put in back of the bag. As she descended a stairway, she put it in the bag.

Shortly after the store opened one morning, a young woman arrived carrying an empty hat bag. She placed two sofa pillows into it.

The manner in which a man stood and watched everyone in the lingerie section before he entered was the reason for his being watched. After a few minutes he walked to a counter, picked up an empty bag from the supply, then as he left the section he picked up a box of panties. As he went up a stairway he placed the box in the bag.

Stores sometimes present the opportunity for thieves to steal merchandise without having to wrap or conceal it. This merchandise is usually packages that have been wrapped for delivery or boxed stock, often a group of boxes tied together and left unattended in a remote area. The thieves are often narcotic addicts who search for quantities of merchandise.

While the lights were being turned off, after the closing bell, a man walked through the electrical appliance section carrying a poorly tied box and a "bad" bag. After circling a counter several times, he rolled up the cord of an electric mixer. The buyer came from the office and asked if he wished attention. His answer was negative and he left the section. Instead of leaving the store he proceeded to an enclosed stairway, walked up part of a flight, waited minutes, then returned to the appliances, where he put the box over the mixer and then put it under his coat.

One young man who was arrested stealing expensive art objects readily agreed to demonstrate various methods he used to steal. While looking at a bracelet held prominently in his right hand, he slyly slipped another one into his left coat pocket. While looking at a book, he slipped another one under his coat. He wore his shirt unbuttoned and expensive bric-a-brac went into his open shirt. The actions of his right hand were always conspicuous enough to detract attention from what the left hand was doing.

Watch Out For That Thief,[1] a pamphlet published by the Store Management Group, N.R.D.G.A., contains a number of photographs illustrating shoplifting methods.

A question by one of the critics of this writing was: "Might this be too instructive for the general public?" I think not. The intrinsically honest reader will not be stimulated to shoplift. The professional already devotes his entire time and energy to larceny and will learn nothing new from this writing. In fact he could add a crowning touch to it.

My experience indicates that the weaklings, even juveniles, who succumb to temptation in shops, originate ideas of their own for stealing. They may also learn from daily newspaper writings and magazine articles which appear frequently.[2]

If my writing is instructive to the general public, it will also be informative to store employes, a part of the general public. Customers, as well as employes, sometimes spot shoplifters, and by informing store personnel of their suspicions, help to reduce loss.

---

[1] *Watch Out For That Thief*, published by the Store Management Group, National Retail Dry Goods Association (now, The National Retail Merchants Association, 100 W. 31st Street, New York 1, N.Y.).

[2] Shoplifting, by Spencer Klaw, *Harper's Bazaar,* September, 1950.

Shady Ladies, by Norma Lee Browning, *The Chicago Tribune,* August 22, 1948.

Stop That Shoplifter!, by Stewart Sterling, *Saturday Evening Post,* October 22, 1949.

Anybody Might Be A Shoplifter, Amelia de Santis as told to Henry La Cossitt, *Bluebook,* March 1954.

How Do You Know A Shoplifter?, by Croswell Bowen, *Pageant,* May, 1956.

Chapter 5
KLEPTOMANIA—WHAT IS IT?

KLEPTOMANIA is a term that is often misused in discussions on shoplifting, especially when it is used only to describe the habitual thief.

Many times I have heard the story, which has also appeared in print, of a wealthy woman, a kleptomaniac, who would pilfer merchandise, which the store would charge to her account, on authorization of her husband. I had never been able to identify the store or the locale. In fact, it would be almost impossible for most stores to make such arrangements. The kleptomaniac might be spotted in some thefts, but more than likely she would evade detection. She must be apprehended in the theft the same as any other person.

> Kleptomania. This is a term applied to an irresistible impulse to steal. Usually the stealing is particularly foolish, the stolen articles have no particular value for the thief and the stealing is often done in a childish and silly manner. Wealthy women, who have no need for anything, will take articles from department stores. One man, whose wife had such a compulsion, made an arrangement with the stores frequented by his wife, whereby they would send him the bills for the things that his wife took.[1]

Probably the most typical case of kleptomania first came to my attention shortly after entering protection work.

It was reported to me that an exceptionally well and expensively dressed, distinguished and matronly-appearing woman had been observed to steal several inexpensive articles. On two other occasions she had attempted to secure refunds on items for which she had no sales check; they were taken from her and the refund refused. She made no further claim for them, so instructions were

---

[1] Morgan, John J. B., Ph.D., Associate Professor of Psychology, Northwestern University, *The Psychology of Abnormal People*, Longmans, Green and Co., New York, London, Toronto. 1928, p. 294.

given to the operators to apprehend her the next time she lifted anything, regardless of the price.

Within a few days she was caught stealing several items with a value of about $12. She admitted previous thefts and gave assurance that it would never occur again. She was advised to discuss her problem with her husband, a man of prominence.

Several months later she was again apprehended shoplifting. On this occasion she dropped to her knees and begged and pleaded that her husband should not be called. Anything would be promised to avoid it. He was called.

The husband was critical of the fact that he had not been notified of the first episode because he had subsequently been embarrassed when she had taken something from the home of friends. I was blamed for his embarrassment over this, but after some discussion the couple left to visit a psychiatrist.

Some time later I learned that the same woman had been taken to court for shoplifting in another store but that was not her last experience.

Some months elapsed and she was once more apprehended, and again was taken to court. Her psychiatrist appeared in court at the time of this trial, and informed the judge that the defendant had refused to cooperate with his efforts at treatment and had been sent to a sanitarium by her husband. While there she had pilfered articles from the rooms of other patients which caused her dismissal.

I credit the judge with a wise decision. He continued the case for one year with the stipulation that she was to cooperate with the doctor; that if she failed to do so he was to report to the court, her case would then be advanced on the docket, and she would be sentenced to serve a year's term. The doctor gave a favorable report and she was discharged when the case was finally heard a year later.

I chanced to meet this woman once since. She was in the store with a friend but stopped to assure me that she had overcome her problems and would never again meet me under the previous circumstances. This last meeting was many years ago and I am confident that if she had been in any trouble since, that is in our city, I would have heard of it.

Dictionaries define kleptomania as an insane, irresistible, or uncontrollable propensity to steal and a kleptomaniac as one so afflicted. Simple, but after having talked to thousands of shoplifters the question arises: "Is this definition reasonably sufficient to recognize or identify any one shoplifter as a kleptomaniac?" Further study is necessary.

Kleptomania, in the index of *Encylopedia of Criminology*, refers the reader to "Perversion."

> The object stolen has a symbolic meaning to the offender. It is the act, however, rather than the object which invests the offense with a value to the offender. . . . Punishment of these individuals is ineffective as it emotionalizes the act and, therefore, makes it all the more exciting to the doer. While these cases are of great interest to the student of abnormal pathology, they are relatively rare and from the point of view of the police do not constitute a great source of annoyance. For every case of true kleptomania there are perhaps fifty cases of outright shoplifting where the motive is pure greed and gain.[2]

My opinion would be that there are hundreds of cases of outright shoplifting to one of kleptomania. Many of them because of delinquency, some by confirmed criminals, others because of some emotional state other than a mania. Dr. Arieff[3] states that many shoplifters are not thieves at all. They are people with more or less normal personality in whom shoplifting occurs as an accident due to some emotional stress or strain.

Mr. Snider quotes Dr. Arieff as saying these persons have no relationship to the professional shoplifter who practices the art as a premeditated means of making a living or the kleptomaniac who has a compulsion for stealing.

Dr. Irving S. Cutter, in an article, "How Kleptomaniacs Get That Way" says:

> Not many instances of true kelptomania are seen by the police. Reported cases of theft for the most part are intentional, deliberate, and actuated by the profit motive. Nevertheless, in certain instances it is possible to charge the episode to the mental makeup of the culprit. Curiously enough, women are more

---

[2] Edited by Branham, Vernon C., M.D., and Kutash, Samuel B., Ph.D., *Encyclopedia of Criminology*, Philosophical Library, New York, 1949, p. 308-309.

[3] Snider, Arthur J., Staff Science Writer, *Chicago Daily News*, July 2, 1947.

subject to the tendency than men. Males who develop the habit are likely to present many feminine characteristics.

Instead of calling these episodes "compulsive," why not look upon them as "compensations" or "substitutes" for hidden longings? The articles purloined are desired not perhaps for their intrinsic value, but to hide away and gloat over.[4]

Cases of this kind will be found occasionally. A woman of the upper socio-economic class, usually past middle age, will claim to be at a complete loss to explain why she shoplifted. She will readily admit previous thefts and even identify the articles that she possesses. The articles may be found neatly packed and well hidden in the home. One very fine woman carefully explained that the articles she had finically preserved were far too inexpensive for her use. She had numerous pieces of stolen costume jewelry but never wore any other than precious metals and stones.

Dr. Theodore R. Van Dellen says:

> Obsessions are innocent, altho they may become so deep as to dominate the mind. In kleptomania for example, there is no motive for stealing. The victim may be wealthy and she never knows what to do with the loot. But stealing a bottle of perfume or a strand of beads when the clerk's back is turned seems to relieve her inner tension. She may throw the item away or take it home and never use it. She lives in fear of getting caught but her will is paralyzed and she cannot help herself.[5]
>
> The conditions grouped under the heading of manias are characterized by the fact that the patient engages in acts that are unlawful, in spite of the fact that he is reluctant to commit them and knows that he thereby runs the danger of arrest and punishment. Such patients behave and act well and apparently normally when they are not engaged in these activities. . . . (Kleptomania is listed among the group of manias.) . . . The objects stolen are either not of much use to these individuals, or they do not have to be obtained through theft. . . . Sometimes a person steals objects which have a sexual significance for him; . . ."[6]

[4] Cutter, Dr. Irving S., *The Chicago Tribune*, 1942.
[5] Van Dellen, Dr. Theodore R., Do You Have a Phobia? *The Chicago Tribune*, 1955.
[6] Maslow, A. H., Ph.D., Brooklyn College, and Mittelmann, Bela, M.D., New York Post-Graduate Dispensary Service Of Neurology and Psychiatry, *Principles Of Abnormal Psychology*, Harper & Brothers, Publishers, New York, 1941, p. 394.

The writer of the following letter no doubt suffered from a "mania" which a psychiatrist might have diagnosed as kleptomania:

> I wish I knew how to express my appreciation for your kindness to me last Saturday. I needed such an incident to occur to cause me to realize the seriousness of my mania—if it may be called that.
>
> Perhaps a psychiatrist can help me to understand how a person of normal wholesome home environment with more than the average amount of education and materialistic wealth could develop such a mania.
>
> I felt like one awakening from a nightmare that Saturday evening. In my subconscious mind I felt that since what I took was later given to others more needy—rather than kept for my own use, that my actions weren't so awful. I realize the fallacy of my reasoning now—thanks to you.
>
> The other gentleman who talked with me Saturday asked me how I could rest at night with such deeds on my conscience. I will admit that such is difficult for me. When the realization "hit me" later—after last Christmas mania, I thought of doing something desparate to myself rather than to continue to disgrace myself and my parents. I would have sought the aid of a psychiatrist last Christmas—but after a short period I was back to my normal self.
>
> It has been a painful lesson, but I am glad it was learned now rather than later.
>
> Thank you many times again for the understanding you gave me when I so needed it. I sincerely hope that I will not misuse the trust you have shown me.
>
> Sincerely,
Signed _____

This woman has not repeated her thefts from stores, to my knowledge. I am convinced that many other similar cases, of persons with a mania, have been brought to a realization of their folly without having been prosecuted.

Other women, apprehended shoplifting, have readily admitted an emotional upset due to sexual problems. They have even asked for advice and were always referred to their doctor.

The laws do not always recognize that a sex crime may be committed by a person who is not a sexual deviate, or that crimes which are not sexual in nature may have a basis in serious sexual psychopathology. . . . The theft of jewelry, in kleptomania, may be a substitute for sexual activity.[7]

. . . The strong relationship between sexual pathology and such criminal acts as kleptomania and pyromania should be borne in mind.[8]

. . . We are too apt to be satisfied when it appears that a crime has been committed because of apparent gain, but this not always is the real motive. Indeed, in delving into the causes of certain types of stealing, such as shoplifting, or . . . , one finds motives which are beyond any comprehension of the culprit. One may find that stealing, which takes the form of a kleptomania, is an expression of a disguised wish for sexual intercourse.[9]

. . . Thus in a case of kleptomania, for instance, the offender should be referred to a psychiatrist with psychoanalytic experience rather than imprisoned. However, such a recommendation depends entirely upon the attitude of the court and upon the type of case. . . .[10]

In interpreting what takes place unconsciously in the mind of a pyromaniac or a kleptomaniac, one may say that the desires of the id and a desire for punishment alternate, the obsessional neurosis acting as a defense against aggressive impulses. The conflict is internalized while the person's superego keeps the conflict back, with the result that he has to act out his inclination. Deep in the unconscious is a forbidden wish such as a sexual one.[11]

The true kleptomaniac belongs in the impulse-ridden and compulsive group. Female kleptomaniacs are believed to be sexually unsatisfied women with tremendous hostility.[12]

Who for instance, can doubt that kleptomania, as we see it

---

[7] MacDonald, John M., M.D., Assistant Professor of Psychiatry, University of Colorado School of Medicine, Assistant Medical Director, Colorado Psychopathic Hospital, *Psychiatry and the Criminal*, Charles C Thomas, Publisher, Springfield, Illinois. 1958, p. 144.

[8] *Ibid.*, p. 146.

[9] Abrahamsen, David, M.D., Department of Psychiatry, Columbia University, *Crime and The Human Mind*, Columbia University Press, New York, 1944, p. 21.

[10] *Ibid.*, p. 92.

[11] *Ibid.*, p. 107.

[12] Karpman, Benjamin, M.D., Chief Psychotherapist, Saint Elizabeths Hospital, Washington, D.C., *The Sexual Offender and His Offenses*, Julian Press, Inc., New York, 1954, p. 138.

clinically, is a symptomatic expression of a full-fledged neurosis? Yet if coming under observation of a psychiatric hospital it is likely to be diagnosed Psychopathic Personality, with or without psychosis.[13]

There is the widest possible difference between predatory theft and kleptomania.[14]

Dr. Karpman states that kleptomania may be related to frustrated love, jealousy, rivalry, frigidity, homosexuality, fetishism, etc. My interpretation of his writings would be that kleptomania is clearly an emotional disorder in which feelings for compulsive acts, without objective evidence of disease, dominate the personality; however, it is a condition to be determined by psychiatry.

My motive in elaborating on this subject is to furnish a better understanding of some actions of persons that are encountered in store protection. Fortunately for store protection personnel, "not many instances of true kleptomania are seen by the police." In spite of that, there are many instances which appear obvious to a layman, that some people apprehended stealing, border on kleptomania.

Frequently a shoplifter, when being released, will be advised to consult a doctor or a psychiatrist. This is usually done because some apparent emotional disturbance appears to be evident during an interview.

One young woman, a senior in an out-of-town university, on a week-end trip to Chicago, was caught shoplifting. A letter from her explained her problem:

> *I have not forgotten I promised to inform you of the results of my psychiatric treatments since our talk in Chicago before Thanksgiving.*
>
> *It is the opinion of my psychiatrist that I have an aversion toward my mother—developing since early childhood. He believes that I have been unconsciously trying to hurt her as a form of retaliation.*
>
> *Mother's recent opposition toward my marriage now climaxes her many past oppositions. By bringing disgrace to her, I unconsciously felt I would feel free to join my fiance. I realize the one-sided reasoning which prompted my actions—yet I am con-*

---

[13] *Ibid.*, p. 397.
[14] *Ibid.*, p. 505.

fused. I never thought I would intentionally hurt anyone.

As confused as I am, I am sure that I'll never attempt to free myself from mother's control in the manner I previously attempted.

I do want to thank you once again for your kindness to me when I most needed it.

Sincerely,

Signed _____

Joseph Jastrow, Ph.D., LL.D., in *Piloting Your Life,* relates that:

> High Grade Individuals may show kleptomania as almost an isolated symptom of hysteria. They may steal useless things and pay no attention to them after they get them. The ordinary motives do not apply; many kleptomaniacs can well afford to buy whatever they want.
>
> Stealing in these cases is plainly a symptom of abnormal condition; how abnormal one cannot say. Kleptomania may be an episode in youth; it may be repeated; it may occur once and never again. When repeated and associated with other neurotic symptoms, the diagnosis is clear.
>
> As to cure that depends on the details of the case. You don't cure the symptom; you improve the general condition of the patient by all means at hand. The change in the entire mode of life is helpful. Many a kleptomaniac will steal in one surrounding and not in another. It is by no means a hopeless condition; wise care and precaution will diminish the tendency, as will removal of the temptation. Responsibility remains a matter of degree. The management of kleptomania consists in so arranging the environment and the patient's relation to it that this type of behavior just falls out of the picture. The temptation is more and more easily resisted, then ceases to be one. . . .
>
> The breaking down of that resistance must be accomplished before the kleptomania yields.[15]

In trying to associate individuals with the scientific definitions for kleptomania, I am reminded of one woman. She is a member of a prominent family and is apparently comfortably situated, but she has been apprehended shoplifting on several different occasions. At one time she had been under suspicion for several days prior to being caught in the act of stealing. She admitted

---

[15] Jastrow, Joseph, Ph.D., LL.D.: *Piloting Your Life,* Greenberg Publisher, Inc., New York, 1930, p. 141-142.

the theft of the item for which she was originally suspected, but insisted that, because she had no use for it, she had dropped the shopping bag and the contents in the alley near her apartment hotel, while on her way home.

Psychiatric findings in research by Mary Cameron, Ph.D.,[16] show something of the personal characteristics of some of 873 women who were officially charged in the Municipal Court of Chicago, with shoplifting. Of these women, 57 were referred by the court for examination by the court psychiatric service. Twelve of the women were found to be committable to the Chicago Psychopathic Hospital for further examination and for disposition. Since this is the procedure regularly followed with suspected psychotics, there thus seems to be a relatively insignificant relationship between shoplifting and actual or probable psychosis.

Of the remaining 45, of the 57 referred to the psychiatrist, 2 were found to have no specific psychiatric disability; 2 were not examined; 2 were reported as showing no evidence of central nervous system pathology; and 1 was diagnosed as a simple mental deficient. Four others were narcotic addicts who had reached this court instead of being booked in the narcotics court. The range of the psychiatric diagnoses of the remaining 34 is as follows: involutional reaction, 8; reactive depression, 4; emotional instability, 2; emotional immaturity, 6; compulsive neurosis, 4; adult maladjustment, 2; psychoneurosis with alcoholism, 2; schizoid personality, 1; hysterical with fugue states, 1; paranoid trend, 1; inadequate personality, 1; kleptomania with simple adult maladjustment, 1.

On the basis of these findings it appears that psychiatric diagnosis did not reveal any characteristic trends of personality deviation among those shoplifters who were examined.

Any decision in connection with the disposition of any case, to be made by store personnel, should be made on the basis of other factors and not on the assumption that the individual is a kleptomaniac.

[16] Cameron, Mary, Ph.D.: Thesis submitted to the Faculty of the Graduate School in partial fulfillment of the requirements for the degree, Doctor of Philosophy, in the Department of Sociology, Indiana University, July 1953, p. 118-119.

Chapter 6
EMPLOYE THEFTS

FIDELITY and Surety Companies have issued statements, at different times, estimating that employe dishonesty costs American business over a half billion dollars a year. These estimates usually cover fidelity losses that have been reported. It would be impossible to estimate the unknown amount of pilferage of merchandise, from stores, by employes.

> One eastern drug chain had a $1,400,000 inventory loss in six months so the management used lie detectors on its 1,400 employes. It was found that nearly three-fourths of the employes had been helping themselves to merchandise and petty cash. Such surveys seem to indicate that small-scale theft, cheating, lying is prevalent in about 60 per cent of the population.[1]

"Holds Employes Cause 75% of Inventory Shrinkage,"—headlines in one article; however, my guess would be that this figure is too high, even though the non-delinquent as well as the delinquent plays a part in the calculated risk that stores must take with employes.

What are the calculated risks, and how do the employes explain their actions after they have been caught stealing?

> I started taking small stuff at first. That was about 3 or 3½ years ago, maybe 4. We had a Birthday Club in the section and we always gave gifts to the girls. I would buy them and one birthday, I think it was my own, I bought an article and the salesperson put two in the box. She told me after she handed me the box—then it got to be more and more. She gave things to me and I gave things to her.

Another employe, a wife and mother, said:

> When I stole dresses, I wrapped them around my body,

[1] Laird, Donald A.: Psychology and the Crooked Employe, *The Management Review*, April 1950.

under my clothing and walked out of the store with them concealed in that way. The other items, such as electric irons, I would conceal in a shopping bag under groceries and fruits. The smaller items, stockings, I would put in my purse.

A young woman wrote:

> I've been doing a lot more composed thinking the last couple of days than I had been able to do previously. I'm writing this letter as I seem to feel pretty tongue-tied in your presence and if I get some of these things down and off my mind I feel I'll be better able to cooperate with you when I come in next Tuesday.
>
> I've not admitted two of the names you presented mainly to avoid involving anymore innocent people than I already have—and also because of the tremendous shame I feel on having to tell my friends how I have used them. As one of them said that was my worst offense—using them without their knowing just what was involved.
>
> The friends I have confessed to have reacted marvellously tho—I know you'll find this hard to believe—but I gave so much stuff away—I amaze myself—but I got a tremendous kick out of being able to do so much for my friends. Of course, they wondered and I invented various stories—that I had connections in the sections that gave me things at cost and less. I refused to accept payment for anything. These people had done favors for me—I get rides from some of them and they won't accept gas money—another does alterations and all accepted packages for me—and I used this as my excuse for giving them things, I could only have sold things to strangers and I did not want to run that risk, and I could not make a profit off my friends. I have an excessively generous nature—and with me it's a vice—because I usually wind up getting stepped on—And of course this time I was generous with what was not mine, . . .
>
> Sincerely,
Signed _____

The employe had been questioned about a number of forged shippers that were being investigated. In order to prevent suspicion, they had been sent to various of her friends, at different addresses.

Employes who steal quantities of merchandise other than wearing apparel, may hoard it. Recoveries may consist of bric-a-brac, linens, silverware, glassware, appliances, or other items.

Employe Thefts

Other respected employes, who have been apprehended stealing, have been just as generous in sharing what was not theirs. In contrast, some have hoarded stolen merchandise.

A watchman observed an employe, whose work required that he enter the store early, slip some boys' pants under the bib of his overalls. This man's working hours also ended an hour and a half before the store closed, which would present an opportunity for him to leave the premises without a pass-out on packages that he might carry out. Because of a series of night time losses that had been reported, and because this theft made him a likely suspect, he was asked for a written authorization permitting representatives of the company to search his home.

He lived in a neat story and a half bungalow and in the upper half story were rows and stacks of wooden chests. They were well made, varnished inside and out, and each one had a lock on it. Neatly packed away in these chests were hundreds of articles, worth thousands of dollars. Among them were 28 watches, stolen from a locked case that had been forced open.

There were 4 cameras, 3 binoculars, 15 sun glasses, 6 lighters, 9 flashlights, 25 wallets, 22 clocks, 11 scissors, 14 pocket knives, and many other articles. Personal tools belonging to fellow workers were also found in his home. He had hoarded evidence that cleared up many mysteries.

Another employe, who was both generous and miserly with stolen merchandise, committed acts of fraud to gain the good will of both customers and employes who depended upon her for favors. Many stolen articles were given as gifts; also, much was hoarded. She accepted complete responsibility for her acts, but could give no explanation except the one that Satan influenced her, and that she would now have to account to God for her errors. She did state, "I merged my identity with that of the company to the extent of thinking what was theirs, was mine."

Some employes will steal merchandise for resale. One woman was stopped while leaving the store with a very large package which had a pass-out of a small purchase attached. She had taken her purchase to a stockroom and added to it four boxes of shirts and six dozen handkerchiefs. She stated that whenever she carried a package out, she would ask her supervisor for permission to leave about ten minutes before her regular quitting time, but that she didn't always carry her own packages. Two other girls who worked in the same area would often carry the packages out, because they were friendly. They apparently did not know that the packages contained stolen merchandise. The woman had been selling shirts for $1 each.

A newspaper article reported that the police, acting on information supplied by officials of the store, raided three apartments and seized part of the merchandise which had been stolen from one of the suburban stores.

Information had been received that a man was selling hosiery, with store price tags, to restaurant waitresses and patrons, in a certain neighborhood. From the description of the man, we were able to spot him, but could not identify him as an employe. He was followed to his hotel where we rented an adjoining room until we were able to identify his associates.

At the time the police recovered the merchandise, they arrested the peddler, his girl friend, and an employe of the company.

While being interrogated at the police station, the employe stated that his first theft was about two months earlier. He had taken "a couple of pairs of hose" for his girl friend. He took them out of the boxes and concealed them under his shirt.

His friend, the peddler, happened to be at the girl's apartment at the time he presented them, and made an offer to buy some. The employe then took a few more every day for about seven weeks and his friend bought them all.

Then an offer was made to purchase a quantity of hose. Plans were made to get them out of the store. The friend suggested that he have his girl friend drive a rented car to the store at 2:00 p.m. on a specified date.

The employe said:

> I started to work on the hose on the 10th of the month and on the 14th I took them out. This is the way I got them out; I removed the hose from the original boxes and packed them in a large carton. I burned the original boxes while the porter and the stock boy were out for lunch. On the 14th, at exactly 2:00

o'clock, his girl friend was on the lower floor of the store. As soon as she saw me, and I saw her, she walked up the stairs and I followed with the box containing 760 pairs of hose. I placed them in the car and she drove away.

Further questioning:

Q. Do we understand that there were two boxes?
A. Yes there were.
Q. We have one box, taken from your friend's room, which we will show you now. Was this one of the cartons you packed and delivered to the car?
A. Yes.
Q. How do you know?
A. I work around that kind of merchandise all day and that's why I know it is the same box.

He had been informed by the police that he was under arrest and that any statement made might be used against him in any future criminal proceedings, and that he did not have to make a statement, or answer any questions, unless he desired to do so.

A number of employes of the store had been released for thefts shortly before this man was arrested. In a conversation I had with him, he said, "Practically every employe under the previous management was stealing and that was proven by those that were caught. I think the reason was that the manager was not strict enough with the employes. He was a fine fellow to work for but he did not check on his employes and actually placed temptation before them."

While under arrest in the police station this man was disturbed about disappointing the new store manager and did not want to see him. He seemed to think that the new manager thought "well of him," and that the employes worked better than they had for the previous manager.

The employes he referred to as having previously been released were apprehended because of anonymous information. While some anonymous information may be unfounded and occasionally it may be from a "crank," none can be ignored.

Copies of a document had been mailed to "Secret Service," the Store Manager, the Auditing Division, and the Superintendent.

Employe Thefts

To Whom Shall Come These Present Greetings

That, We, students of _____ University, specializing in Business Administration, engaged in research work in larceny and theft among employes, found much valuable information in the _____ store.

That, We being of sound mind and disposing memories, and being desirous of giving payment in consideration for the aforesaid information, do now and hereby bestow graciously and convey voluntarily the riches of these experiences.

That, . . . compose a theft ring, which in the course of a year would make considerable shortage in inventories.

The information was equally graciously received, worked on, and verified. The results, no doubt, contributed to a reduced shrinkage the following inventory period.

A "ring" or group of employes practicing petty thievery will be discovered from time to time. The following occurred during the middle 1930's. There have been others since then in which the merchandise stolen was much more valuable, but the theme of generosity among friends, with the property of others, is always the same. The participants of this one "ring" can only be identified by symbols A through Y, a total of twenty-five.

A and B were first questioned on a Saturday after B had given a box of candy to A.

When A returned on the following Monday she made the following statement:

> I have felt very badly since last Saturday, about what I have been doing myself and about what I know other employes to be doing. My husband has been very fine to me and very considerate and he has advised me to do everything I can now to try to clear up this situation. I have thought everything over very clearly, and what I am about to tell you, I know to be the absolute facts. I do not want to make any statements that may implicate any innocent parties. I also am satisfied that some of the statements I make only confirm information which you already have.
>
> When I started working for the company I became acquainted with a woman C, who lives in my neighborhood. I had never stolen anything from the company until one day, about noon, C

sent a package to me by a friend of hers. I do not know the woman's name but she comes in on her lunch hour to see C. I was very much surprised to receive this package, and at that time did not know what to do with it. Since then I have worked with C and I know that she is helping herself to merchandise and gives considerable to her friends to carry out of the store. I have also come to the store when I was not working and selected merchandise from C and have given her some money which she would ring up, but this would not be for the full value of the merchandise.

After having accepted stolen merchandise from C, it became easy for A to follow the pattern of systematic criminal behavior practiced by her associates. Later, an employe, D, made a normal purchase from A, but chanced to remark that she would like to buy more than one article but did not have the money. A explained that she felt very sorry for D, and gave her more than she paid for, because she appeared to be a poor person. A admitted giving D merchandise on several other occasions.

The two who were first questioned on the previous Saturday, became acquainted when B went to A, one day, and said that she was a friend of C. From that day until they were apprehended they had been giving each other merchandise.

A and C were working together one day and, while C was at lunch, E selected merchandise and asked that it be held. A saw C give the merchandise to E later that day.

F and G were identified as being good friends of C who gave each other merchandise and A had received things from F through C.

A observed C ring up a small amount, not the full price, for H, and had also been told that F and H were good friends and gave articles from their respective sections to each other.

I and C gave each other merchandise. I also carried packages out of the store for J. K had worked with A and carried out stolen things.

L and M had worked with A and L got a package from M, who had retained a cash register check from a previous sale, which she put in the package. That same day a fountain pen was found and a floorman put it in a drawer. It disappeared and *L* was suspected of taking the pen. When one of the men came to investigate, *L* became very confused and later said, "Well, anyway I have a check in my package."

A said that when she worked in the candy section she would give over weight to most of the girls from the store, who would buy from her. She thought this practice was general with most of the girls in the candy section at that time.

B admitted giving candy to and receiving merchandise from *A, C, E,* and *G*. She also had the same arrangement with twelve other employes, symbols *N* through *Y*. *B* stated that the first she knew of the free exchange practice among employes was when *Y*, then an ex-employe, told her about *A* and *Q* and those two told her of others.

One woman who had worked in the store for some years prior to a second marriage returned to work for a Christmas season. The following April, she came to the store posing as an employe, a personal shopper, and obtained merchandise, totaling $60, from various sections, by presenting fraudulent sales checks. She claimed that she had never stolen during the previous years she worked for the store. "I think the reason may be due to my being in the menopause, plus the fact that the idea was thrown right into my lap, due to the lack of interest shown by the section personnel. Also, when I was told that there was no more work for me, the salesbook was not taken away from me; I was allowed to keep it in my locker."

Another ex-employe caught stealing: "I never stole anything while working here but I would come in to eat in the employes' lunch room and see some of the gang. It was then that I got the idea. It kept building up and building up. I hadn't thought much about being caught or I wouldn't be sitting here; it seemed easy. I didn't realize I was a crook until I was brought into the office this morning; then I realized what I had done. I never did anything wrong before; I was in the navy four years; I am married and take care of my wife. I don't play around; I don't gamble; I drink moderately; I guess the only reason was that I was tempted."

If these employes, or ex-employes, had been true professional criminals, they would not have cooperated to the same extent that they did after being apprehended.

Numerous other seemingly non-delinquent employes have been tempted. Circumstances necessitate prosecution of some employes, such as the one who sold hosiery to the peddler; others can be discharged, and are sure to benefit from their experiences, as the letter dated December 21st, from a young man indicates:

> *I have been wanting to drop you a few lines for the past few days and offer my heartfelt thanks for your most wonderful kindness and consideration you gave myself and the others involved in the recent "mess" we put ourselves into.*
>
> *It is true that we were guilty in all accounts. Could we deny it? We did deserve a lot more in the form of punishment, that is true, but as I said the torment that went through my heart and conscience was worse than any physical punishment could impart. It mystifies me why the mind goes off in such a way and wrongful deeds are committed even though the wrong is well understood.*
>
> *Please express my thanks to all your colleagues who were assigned to this case. They had a job to do, and besides doing a wonderful job, they were human beings and most understanding when I talked to them.*
>
> *Your thoughtfulness will certainly be a great attribute towards all involved towards a Merry Christmas. You can imagine how the parents would feel to have their offspring sitting in the Bastille watching the world celebrate HIS Birthday through barred windows. Unawares to those parents, they also are thankful to you.*
>
> *I hope and pray that you all have a most joyful holiday season and that all which is deserving to you will come to you in the New Year and all the years that follow.*
>
> *Again, thanks from the bottom of my heart.*
> *Humbly yours,*
> *Signed* _____

Store owners and supervisors do have a responsibility along with protection for enforcing preventive programs. Correct, complete controls are necessary, but they are no better than supervision which should be disciplinary, but fair.

Prevention is a logical policy to use in dealing with crime. Punishment and other methods of treatment are, at best, methods of defense. It is futile to take individual after individual out of the situations which produce criminals and permit the situations to remain as they were.[2]

[2] Sutherland, Edwin H.: *Principles of Criminology*—3rd Edition, J. B. Lippincott Co., Chicago, Philadelphia, New York, 1939, p. 614.

Chapter 7
PICKPOCKETS

"The Bhamptas, a tribe whose home is in the Decan, work all over India. The Bhampta is a marvellously skillful pickpocket and railway thief. He frequents fairs, landing places, bazaars, temples—any place, in fact, where there is a crowd. The children are trained to crime from their earliest childhood, so it is not wonderful that they should become very expert and be always on the lookout for prey."[1]

IN MEXICO CITY tourists are cautioned to be alert to pickpockets, frequently skillful youngsters.

A report from Tokyo, Japan, estimated losses to pickpockets in excess of $45,000,000 a year.

The Chicago Tribune Press Service reports a "finishing school" for shoplifting and pocket picking, discovered by police of Naples, Italy. Girls learned to become expert pickpockets by practicing on dummies with clothes fitted with little bells, and specially built mouse traps in the pockets. The girls were trained to pick out the wallets without getting their fingers caught in the traps, and without making any of the bells ring.

Pickpockets also operate in Washington, D.C., New York, Chicago, and in other communities, both large and small, in the United States. I have never seen statistics on losses to pickpockets, in any American city, but I would think that their take is not nearly so large as Tokyo, because of our police system.

Pickpockets do travel from city to city, but so do the pickpocket squad specialists of our police departments. Preventive measures are usually taken for any large gathering of people at national or local affairs.

An article in a Washington, D.C., newspaper reported a 55 year old pickpocket arrested at 7th Street and Pennsylvania Ave-

---

[1] Sutherland, Edwin H.: *Principles of Criminology*—3rd Edition, J. B. Lippincott Co., Chicago, Philadelphia, New York, 1939, p. 134.

nue, in the parade crowd, by a visiting member of the Chicago police pickpocket squad.

Another article reported the arrest of a woman in New York for using a hospitalization card she had "lifted." It would appear that she was a novice as the professional pickpocket will seldom retain any identification which can be used against him if arrested. A stolen wallet is usually thrown away with all articles which are easily identified, as soon as the money has been removed.

State fairs, county fairs, race meets, and other large sporting events are often patrolled by police from neighboring cities.

Women are most often the victims of pickpockets in department stores and shops. The reason is that many women, while shopping, carry a purse carelessly. Invariably the victim has carried her purse hanging from a strap over her arm and is also carrying packages, a coat, scarf, or other articles which hides or partially hides her purse from her view.

> The pickpocket moves very slowly usually. He depends on the careless habits of his victims, especially their habit of getting interested in other things and forgetting themselves.[2]

The extensive argot of pickpockets is passed on from crook to crook.

Thieves who "pick a poke" are commonly referred to as "moll-buzzers."

Pickpockets are also called "cannons." The theory of the origin of "cannon' 'is that centuries ago a pickpocket was called a gonnif, the Jewish word for thief. Later the term was abbreviated to "gun" and then to "cannon" to designate a big gun. A female pickpocket who operates upon men is called a "gun-moll."

Some additional criminal-slang of pickpocket activities are:

Lift—To pull or to reef a leather, to pick a pocket or purse.
Fork—To pick pockets with the fingers held straight and stiff.
Kiss the dog—To face the victim.
Bridge—To pick a pocket by reaching around the victim.
Sound—To feel a victim's clothes.
Hustle or **work the shorts**—To operate on street cars.
Give the rush act—To work fast in a crowd.

[2] Wiggams, Albert Edward, D.Sc.: Let's Explore your Mind—*Chicago Daily News*.

Beat a mark—To follow and pick the pockets of a victim.
Cover, shade, stall—To act as an accomplice for a pickpocket.
Hustle, put his back up, secure, set up, throw a hump—To distract a victim or place him in a good position for a pickpocket.

Many more slang terms are used by these criminals.

The best advice to women shoppers is that which is issued by the Chicago Police Department as a warning to Christmas shoppers:

> Don't carry your purse by the strap. It's an invitation to the moll-buzzer to open it and remove the change purse.
> The way to carry your purse is the way a full-back carries the ball.

Pickpockets are rated at the bottom of the scale as the most miserable sort of thieves by other professional thieves. Yet it is difficult to get a victim to sign a complaint after the criminal has been apprehended in the act of picking her purse.

A store employe may sign a loss complaint for store property, but cannot sign a complaint for the loss of personal property of a customer. If he has seen a pickpocket operate, and the victim signs the complaint, he will attend court and testify. If the wallet or money has been recovered, the police will take possession of it until the court hearing.

It is a great satisfaction to receive a letter like this one:

> *The purpose of this letter is to thank you for the splendid cooperation of your personnel in securing for me the return of my wallet, which was stolen from me last Wednesday. Your police officers arrested the thief and followed the matter through a hearing in the Criminal Court, after which the wallet was returned to me. I particularly wish to commend your policewoman, who attended to the matter in court not only with intelligence and dignity but with unusual patience and understanding. I am very grateful to you.*
>
> Signed_____

Pickpockets, like shoplifters, and their attorneys will request repeated continuances of the court hearing in an attempt to discourage the complainant, in hopes that she will fail to return to testify.

Who are the "moll-buzzers" who operate in department stores,

Pickpockets

where do they operate, and what is their take?

They may be male or female, old or young, of any race or color.

A study of 83 loss reports indicated that 11 of the picks were on the flat, meaning in a section or at a counter; the balance, 72, were in elevators where the victim is less likely to realize what is happening if she is jostled during the act.

During the 1930 depression years pickpockets stole $573 from seven persons, in one day in one department store. They do not respect the financial status of the victim. The first loss reported that day was at 12:15 p.m. and the victim's last $2. Other losses were: $6 at 1:30 p.m.; $438 at 3:00 p.m.; $50 at 3:15 p.m.; $60 at 3:50 p.m.; $10 and $7 at 3:55 p.m.

A study of 105 loss reports over a period of time indicates that most picks occur later in the day, when women are more likely to be carrying packages and may be less alert, due to fatigue. From these reports, it was found that from 11:00 a.m. to 12:00 noon six picks occurred; from noon to 1:00 p.m., ten; from 1:00 to 2:00 p.m., thirteen; from 2:00 to 3:00 p.m., nineteen; from 3:00 to 4:00 p.m., nineteen; from 4:00 to 5:00 p.m., twenty-nine; and from 5:00 to 5:30 p.m., nine.

A careful investigation of the pattern of activities indicated by the loss reports, and descriptions of suspects from the victims, will sometimes indicate who the person is that is operating.

An old-timer from Milwaukee would visit Chicago at intervals. When there were indications that she was in the store, all store detectives would be alerted. One December 7th, a detective located her, a well-dressed blond woman, observed her open a woman's purse, and then placed her under arrest.

Seldom does a pickpocket of her experience make a mistake such as she made that day. She had in her possession a watch and checks that had been reported stolen earlier in the day. After identification, the owner signed a complaint and the thief was taken to the police station.

The confidence detail of the detective bureau had decided to give an extra amount of publicity to arrests of pickpockets, made that December, in an effort to protect the public. The city detective who handled the case telephoned his headquarters before leaving the store, and when they arrived at the station, newspaper photographers were waiting to take pictures. All the local papers published her picture and gave the arrest publicity.

The broadcasting companies were also alerted and one popular commentator devoted his allotted time on the air, for two nights, to pickpockets in general, and this one in particular:

> This morning in Felony Court, the case of the City of Chicago versus Louise _____ was continued until December 16th.
>
> Since Louise is only one of twenty names used by this venerable old lady, it would be pretty hard to libel her. Even so, I wouldn't want to repeat the bitter indictment of Louise I heard from a veteran police officer this afternoon. You see, Louise is a "mechanic"—a "wire"—both terms being synonyms for pickpocket. When Louise was apprehended on Monday in a downtown store she was loaded down with—at a conservative estimate—ten thousand dollars worth of diamonds—and sixteen hundred dollars in cash. But those weren't the items that annoyed the indignant policeman. She also had the two week paycheck of a young woman employed at the Hines Veterans Hospital.
>
> Can you imagine her taking the money of a girl who's trying to help the boys who were wounded in the war? Those were only a few of the officer's words.
>
> To the head of the Confidence Detail of the Chicago Police Department, Louise, by that or any other name, is an old acquaintance—if not an old friend. He acknowledges her ability in her profession—if he doesn't admire it.
>
> "She's the last word," he told me, "the top among the woman pickpockets."
>
> The lieutenant has known Louise a long time.
>
> "She's been in and out of prisons since 1914," he told me. I wondered why she went to prison so often if she is, as the lieutenant said, so proficient at her trade.
>
> "Her score is pretty good," he said. "She can make a thousand dollars a day. We had her last year about this time, now we have her again—and that's a pretty good average for her."
>
> Louise's record is a coast-to-coast affair. She's been nabbed in New York City, Los Angeles, and Spokane, Washington. Apparently, though she has a fondness for her native state— Wisconsin. She comes from Milwaukee, and twice in her long and undistinguished career, she has served terms in the state prison at Waupun.
>
> There are plenty of women pickpockets in circulation, and

plenty of men, but there is no really outstanding artist on the male side anymore to compete for Louise's title of master pickpocket.

"The business isn't so good for men anymore," says the lieutenant. "The race track mobs I used to know twenty-five years ago are a thing of the past. Once in a while we run into a bank mob, but they're rare, too. The men pickpockets nowadays work the poor neighborhoods where men are paid in cash and stuff it in a pocket."

I needed a fuller explanation on the term "bank mob." The "bank mob," it seems, is a group that specializes in picking the pockets of bank customers. How do they work? In teams—a mechanic and a stall.

The stall is always the "clumsy yokel." He's the one that bumps into the victim—jostles him around—and makes it easy for the mechanic to go to work without being felt.

On a bank job, though, the function of the stall is to get inside and pick out a likely victim who has just been handed a wad of money by a teller. The stall watches which pocket it goes into and passes the information on to the mechanic.

At this season, according to the lieutenant, women are the major victims of the pickpocket crew. There are two reasons for it. First—people by habit put off their Christmas shopping until the last minute—then get into the downtown area in droves with money in their pocketbooks and their minds on shopping.

The second reason for the ladies receiving the attention of the "mechanic" is because of the short days. On the street, darkness works to the advantage of the pickpocket who has to open a woman's purse and remove a billfold. On the long summer days, it's easier to reef a pocket, particularly a sucker pocket.

Those terms were simple for the lieutenant.

"Reefing" a pocket is what a mechanic does when he removes a billfold from a person's clothing. It's called "reefing" because the professional pickpocket never puts his fingers into a pocket at all. He—or she—actually takes hold of the material of the coat or trousers and works it inside out. The billfold simply drops into his hand.

The "sucker" pocket is the hip pocket, and it's known by the name for obvious reasons. It's the easiest pocket of them all for the experienced "wire" to work on. Yet it's the pocket in which the majority of men habitually carry their "poke"—wallet.

The lieutenant says the side pockets of trousers are much safer than the hip pocket—but the safest pockets of all are an inside vester and a fob. The terms are the lieutenant's, although they're fairly easy to understand—the inside pocket of a vest and the watch pocket—or fob pocket.

But that's for men. It's the ladies of the town who are getting the attention right now. The lieutenant has some sound advice for them, too.

When you carry your bag, never carry it dangling by the handle. Take a lesson from the football players. When you carry your purse, do it as a halfback lugs a football. With your arm around it, close into your side, and your fingers across the clasp or zipper opening. The pickpockets aren't strong-arm robbers. They do their work with professional skill and look with contempt on the muscular purse-snatchers.

The shoulder strap bag may be convenient and attractive, but it's a joy to the mechanics. Since women habitually let the bag hang free, particularly during the in-fighting around a bargain-counter, it's a cinch for the pickpocket. Then, too, says the lieutenant, most of the shoulder bags with the envelope fold that puts the clasp at the lower side of the bag seem to give their owners a sense of false security—but actually, they're as easy to open as those with button clasps on top.

If you must wear a shoulder-strap bag—wear it hanging where you can see it, and keep your hand firmly around it.[3]

In his broadcast the following night Mr. Hurlbut said:

I'm inclined to agree with the lieutenant. I walked down State Street today, paying particular attention to the way the ladies carted their handbags. I'd never thought much about the matter until yesterday's conversation. I was startled by what I saw. At least seventy-five per cent of the ladies I passed between Van Buren and Randolph paid no more attention to their handbags than if they were paper sacks loaded with potato peelings. They held them by the handles and waved them around recklessly as they charged in and out of the crowds. A good many of the girls with the shoulder strap bags had them slung in the back the way we used to wear the gas-mask bag—which, you'll remember from last night—is the wrong way to do it.

I did see a good many ladies, though, who had the handbags close against their sides, under their arms, with their hands

---
[3] Broadcast of Jim Hurlbut, WMAQ, N.B.C., Dec. 8, 1948.

across the clasp—just the way I passed on the recommendation from the head of the con detail. Maybe I was only kidding myself when I decided they all heard the show and were following my advice.

We had no losses reported the balance of that December! Publicity is the last thing that any pickpocket wants. The more publicity that is given, the fewer women will suffer losses.

Louise and her twenty aliases may have been the "venerable old lady" of pickpockets, but one other old lady could challenge her reputation of being "the last word."

Periodically a series of picks would be reported and descriptions of a suspect, given by the losers, were of a grey haired, grandmotherly appearing woman, with diamonds in pierced ears.

The suspect could not be identified as anyone having been arrested in Chicago. Because of long periods of time between her visits, it was apparent that she was from out of town. Then late one day two store detectives spotted a kindly appearing elderly woman, with two large diamonds in her ears, carefully watching and following women who carried purses hanging from their arms.

She made no attempt to open any purses, yet her actions were so typical of a "moll-buzzer" that the detectives followed her from the store, hoping to apprehend her in a crowd at a street car or bus stop, or in another store. She went directly to a bus station, where she purchased a ticket to a fairly small town, some 150 miles away, in another state.

Months later, while I was in New York City, a protection manager of one of the large stores mentioned that they had arrested a clever pickpocket who lived near Chicago, an elderly woman, grey hair, and diamond earrings. She had been convicted and was serving time, but a police identification photograph was secured.

Back in Chicago it was identified as the woman spotted in our store, one who had, no doubt, periodically caused us trouble. A check of the local police files revealed that she had been arrested there twice. The last time was thirty-two years earlier, for picking pockets.

Apparently, once a pickpocket, always a pickpocket; therefore, store protection personnel should know and review police pictures, of pickpockets, often.

Chapter 8

NIMBLE FINGERS, MISCELLANEOUS

"STEALS $23. Has $2,962 in Girdle." An imposing woman, handsome in spite of weighing 170 pounds, was arrested on the complaint of another customer. The customer testified that she had left her purse in a toilet booth of the store, and that, as she came out, the woman went in, locked the door and stayed ten minutes. All this time the customer "banged" on the door, but the woman would not answer. When she came out, the $23 was missing from the purse.

In the case of an argument between customers, the city police are called to interview them. A policewoman searched the accused woman and found a large brown envelope, containing $2,962, pinned in her girdle.

Women have lost purses while in toilet booths to thieves who climb up in an adjoining booth and "fish" the purse over the partition.

Probably one of the strangest coincidences of my career occurred a few years ago. It was truth, stranger than fiction. An out-of-town customer reported the loss of her purse from a toilet she occupied. In addition to money, the purse contained a quantity of valuable jewelry.

Detectives were assigned to work on the case, and a description of the jewelry was taken to give to the Pawn Shop Detail of the Detective Bureau. The loss was also reported to the district police station, and some four hours later, a policewoman came to the office. While describing what had happened, the store detective suggested they go to the women's room. As they approached the booth where the loss occurred, the door opened and a tall, modish, young woman came out.

The city policewoman said, "Hello ——, I have been looking for you." The woman was brought to the protection office because she was recognized from previous arrests for the same type of offense.

On searching her, the policewoman found all of the customer's jewelry.

Another equally fantastic case was reported in the Chicago papers on February 19, 1958. A young woman was arrested by store detectives, who watched her take a pint of chocolate ice cream and some sausage, and go off to a corner to eat them.

Upon searching her purse, where she carried a fork and a spoon, jewelry valued at $9,650 was found. A customer from Michigan had lost her purse containing the jewelry the previous October 17th, in the same store.

The young woman admitted she had found the purse in the store, spent the $150 it contained, and kept the jewelry because she did not know how to go about selling it. She had no permanent address and said she had been sleeping in parked automobiles and railroad stations. In fact, she had been arrested for sleeping in a station, once since she carried the jewels.

Store cash registers are equally interesting to nimble fingered thieves. "Till-tappers" frequent stores, and they are also caught.

"Caught in Loop; Couple Held in Bold Store Thefts."

The above headlined a story of a young couple—parents of three—who worked a bold scheme for three months. The young woman posing as a saleswoman, would open and rifle cash register drawers in different stores, while her husband stood near holding her coat. They were arrested after a saleswoman saw the thief rifling her cash drawer. The couple had stolen more than $850 on at least nine different occasions.

Through cooperative efforts of the Retail Special Service Association, Inc., members in Chicago exchange information on losses, types of thefts, and descriptions of suspects. Often this information, which is passed on to store personnel, results in apprehending thieves wanted by a number of stores.

Here is the tale of another "Till-tapper." Just prior to Christmas a number of cash register losses had occurred in the stores. One day store detectives noticed a man who seemed to have an unusual interest in cash registers. He was followed and city police were called. When the man left the store, a city detective stopped him for questioning. It developed he had a long police record, and had recently dipped his hands into a cash drawer in another store.

When asked why he did not steal in our store, the man said, "I always look for open cash register drawers—it's too risky trying to punch the keys and open registers." The moral of this story for salespeople should be: **At least make a crook work for his money— keep cash register drawers closed when there is no reason for them to be open.**

Because fellow employes have stolen from cash drawers, keeping them closed might prevent temptation for an associate.

Another type of thief will sometimes prowl stores, watching for an opportunity to steal a salesperson's bank or receipts, at closing time. He may await a chance to pick up a money bag or box when a salesperson is not looking, or he might grab money that is being counted, as one did.

One salesperson who suffered a loss said, "From now on I'm going to 'make my bank' well behind the counter. It's just too easy to tempt people by having money and valuables lying around within easy reach." She was right—but she had learned the hard way, by the excitement of suffering a loss, and then attending court as a witness against the thief.

It all started after the closing bell had rung. The salesperson worked at a first floor counter adjoining a down escalator. She was counting out her day's receipts on the counter, when suddenly a hand grabbed the pile of bills. Another woman employe, coming down the escalator on her way home, had spotted a suspicious looking man eyeing the saleswoman counting money, and immediately yelled, "Help! Help! That man stole your money."

The thief, an ex-convict, dope addict, and a Skid-Row citizen, made a leap for an escalator. That leap was his big mistake—the escalator was going up and away from exits! Another employe, 6'1" and weighing 190 pounds, just happened to be coming along and sped up the escalator right behind the thief. He overtook his man at the second floor landing and made a flying tackle that caught the fleeing thief right above the shoe laces. Suddenly, the thief became a very quiet and subdued individual.

The employe who gave the alarm was right behind and she recovered the stolen money from a side coat pocket. She said, "I wasn't worried about that thief trying to prevent my recovering the money. How could he? One man had him around the knees— and a night housekeeper was holding him around the neck." About that time, protection personnel arrived, took charge, and sent the thief to the lock-up.

The cases reported here have more dramatic action than the usual run of purse snatching or till-tapping, but they do point out the need for care in handling money or valuables. Salespeople can be trained to be cautious; it is difficult for a store to train the public.

Chapter 9
NARCOTICS AND ADDICTION

The term "habit-forming narcotic drug" or "narcotic" means opium and coca leaves and the innumerable alkoloids derived therefrom, the best known of these alkoloids, heroin, and codeine, obtained from opium, and cocaine derived from the coca plant; all compounds, salts, preparations, or other derivatives obtained either from the raw material or from the various alkoloids; Indian hemp and its derivatives, compounds, and preparations, and peyote in its various forms.

The term "addict" means any person who habitually uses any habit-forming narcotic drug as defined in this chapter so as to endanger the public morals, health, safety, or welfare, or who is or has been so far addicted to the use of such habit-forming narcotic drugs as to have lost the power of self-control with reference to his addiction.[1]

Dangerous "Thrills." In general, the preliminary introduction of it by a "friend" or "some of the guys," stresses the thought that marijuana is harmless, and that they would be able to take it "for laughs." As the body develops a tolerance for marijuana, they appear to switch naturally to heroin, also through others already using it. This switch is generally when the individual believes he is "different," and smart enough not to be hooked.

The daily dosage seems quickly to mount to between four and six capsules, costing $1.50 to $7.50 each. In the beginning, the youthful addicts invent elaborate stories to obtain money from parents, friends, and relatives. Then comes pilfering of objects within the home. If a high school student, he finds his earnings inadequate to purchase the needed supply of drugs. Generally in the company of another addict, he starts out by robbing news stands, then stripping automobiles, stealing packages from delivery trucks, shoplifting, burglary, purse snatching, and an occasional strong arm robbery. A small percentage become "runners" or "pushers" for the drug peddlers, receiving

---

[1] Section 221, Title 21, Foods and Drugs. The Code of Laws of the United States of America.

one capsule for each four they sell. Girls turn to shoplifting and prostitution.[2]

Prior to World War II, arrests of addicts for shoplifting were infrequent. Those who were arrested were generally middle aged white persons, known to store protection personnel, and readily spotted. There was the case of one well known woman addict, who was seen by one of our detectives to check her coat in a nearby bus station. That indicated that she had an order for a coat. She was followed to our main women's coat section, but she did not take a coat. She went to the coat section of another store and then returned to our basement section, where she stole a coat.

The suggestion to this addict, that she ask the judge to sentence her to a long term so that she could get the cure, evoked the answer: "You get the cure in jail, but when you get out the peddlers find you, give you a free shot, and then you are on again."

Then, the peddlers sought the addicts. Today, it is reversed, the addicts seek the peddlers. A young man, majoring in music in one of the Universities, was arrested shoplifting. He claimed that his addiction was due to his association with the "down beat boys." This chap lived on the far north side of Chicago but traveled to a south side street for his supply of heroin. He would stand on a corner until approached by a peddler or runner. There are "con" rackets here too. At times he would advance the money for a purchase and then be left standing on the corner.

Recently a young man arrested for the theft of phonograph records stated that he "took a bang" in Indianapolis, Indiana on his way home from the United States Public Health Service Hospital, Lexington, Kentucky. His father had arranged for his entrance into the hospital for treatment to cure his habit. It did not take him long to seek a peddler.

Since World War II, there has been a great increase in addicts' shoplifting. Most of them are youths and the majority are black males.

Data from the Crime Prevention Bureau, Chicago, Dr. Lois

---

[2] Higgins, Lois, A.B., M.S.W., LL.D.: The Status of Narcotic Addiction in the United States. *The American Biology Teacher*, Vol. 16, No. 4, April 1954.

Higgins, Director, indicates that there were 6,000 to 7,000 dope addicts in Chicago on July 1, 1951. On July 1, 1948 there were less than 3,000 such unfortunates in this city. As of July 1957 the police files record some 7,100 addicts in the city, yet 9,011 persons were processed through the Narcotic Bureau during the year 1956, and a total of 12,399 cases were disposed of in the Narcotic Court during the same period.

The variation in figures is probably due to the fact that some addicts were arrested more than once, also some addicts processed were not residents of the city. Addicts are required by law to register but all of them do not do so. A number who were arrested shoplifting admitted that they had never registered as addicts. One woman who was arrested said, "They busted me, but only two, of the fifteen I know that are on the stuff, have records."

The annual report of the Chicago Narcotic Bureau shows that of the 9,011 processed, 67 were juveniles, 687 minors, 3,326 were 21 to 25 years of age, 2,897 were 26 to 30 years, 1,147 were 31 to 35 years, and 977 were 36 and over.

During the year 1956 there were 382 addicts in court on shoplifting charges; 214 pickpocket, purse snatching, con game, and check fraud; 475 larceny or attempted larceny; 627 robbery, burglary, or attempted burglary. Any one of these charges could have been problems of the stores.

It is interesting to note that the offense of shoplifting by addicts in Oakland, California, was even greater than in Chicago. The Oakland police department reports 497 shoplifting cases from April to December, 1955, and 442 cases April to December, 1956. Oakland has probably felt the narcotic problem to a greater degree than some cities because it is a port city, and the center of a rapidly growing metropolitan area.

The Oakland police department published a report, "A *New* Approach to the Detection of Narcotic Addiction, Nalline." They, in cooperation with the district attorney and the courts are using Nalline, a narcotic itself, but one antagonistic to opium derivatives, for the detection and control of narcotics addiction. Addicts are a medical problem, however, because they almost invariably resort to crime; the program was undertaken to remove from society, those who cannot control the habit.

It is too early to judge the effectiveness of the therapeutic value of "Nalline," but the indications are that the decrease in shoplifting cases, in Oakland, for 1956 may be due to the program.

The confession of one addict explains the problem that the increase in users has made for retailers. "Most addicts can't make enough money working to pay for the stuff, and they drift into the underworld as boosters, shoplifters, and pickpockets."

The addicts frequently travel in pairs and steal from stockrooms, receiving platforms, or freight elevator areas where quantities of boxed merchandise are available.

During one three-month's period, 31 addicts were arrested in downtown State Street stores alone. It is difficult to estimate the total loss to stores as a result of their thefts. Of this total, 14 were sentenced to one year each, the others for lesser terms. On release from the jail or House of Correction, they will return to stealing from the stores.

The dope problem is not confined to Chicago or Oakland merchants. An article in a Washington, D.C. newspaper stated that a young mother told police that dope was the only accomplice her nimble fingers needed to lift $10,000 in loot from Washington shops. She had been taught the art of lifting by a girl friend, a fellow narcotic.

Her technique was one that professional shoplifters sometimes used. This method is explained as follows: She would remove a dress from a rack, look at it, and place it on a chair. She would then walk away, look around, and when she thought no one was looking, would slip it into a shopping bag or between her coat and dress.

We once arrested a man who stole two blouses from one side of a counter and then walked around to the other side, where he asked for a refund. He stated that he had just been released from jail, had no money, and met a peddler of heroin in a bus station. The peddler had suggested this method for obtaining money and came into the store with him to show him what to do.

Every addict apprehended stealing from, or in stores, should be prosecuted, because he is a prisoner to his habit and is helpless to aid himself.

How is an addict identified? Often he will carry the equipment used to inject the narcotic into his veins. Such equipment will usually consist of an eye dropper with a hypodermic needle attached, a bit of cotton, and a spoon or bottle cap which is smoke blackened underneath and in which the heroin is cooked.

In the absence of the equipment, persons who come into contact with addicts soon learn to recognize physical characteristics indicating the use of narcotics. Questioning often elicits an affirmative answer that the person is, or has been, a user; otherwise, the glistening look in the eyes and dilation of the pupils are an indication. A series of welt-like scars along the veins of the arm are proof that he is on the "junk."

The report of a Senate Judiciary Subcommittee is:

> Illegal dope traffic has trebled since World War II. At the end of the war, there was one addict to every 10,000 persons in the United States, in 1955 there was one to every 3,000. Thirteen percent of all addicts in the country are under 21.
>
> Approximately 50% of all crime in the United States cities, and 25% of all crime in the nation, is attributed to drug addiction.[3]

An addict on a store payroll is a shrinkage risk; therefore, pre-employment physical examinations should aim to prevent the employment of that one in 3,000.

A shoe salesman had been on the payroll for three days when an anonymous telephone call was received from a man, saying the employe, an addict, had approached him to assist in stealing shoes. An investigation proved the addict charge and revealed a past criminal police record. Results: one ex-employe.

Heroin is used by most of the addicts arrested for shoplifting, but marijuana smokers and users of barbiturates, to excess, have also become boosters. One woman, who has probably been picked up in every large store, is the only local shoplifter known to be an opium addict. An officer of the Narcotic Unit, Chicago Police Department, has appraised the cost of her habit to be $2,000 a week. She steals and attempts to secure a cash refund before leaving the store.

[3] *Time,* January 16, 1956.

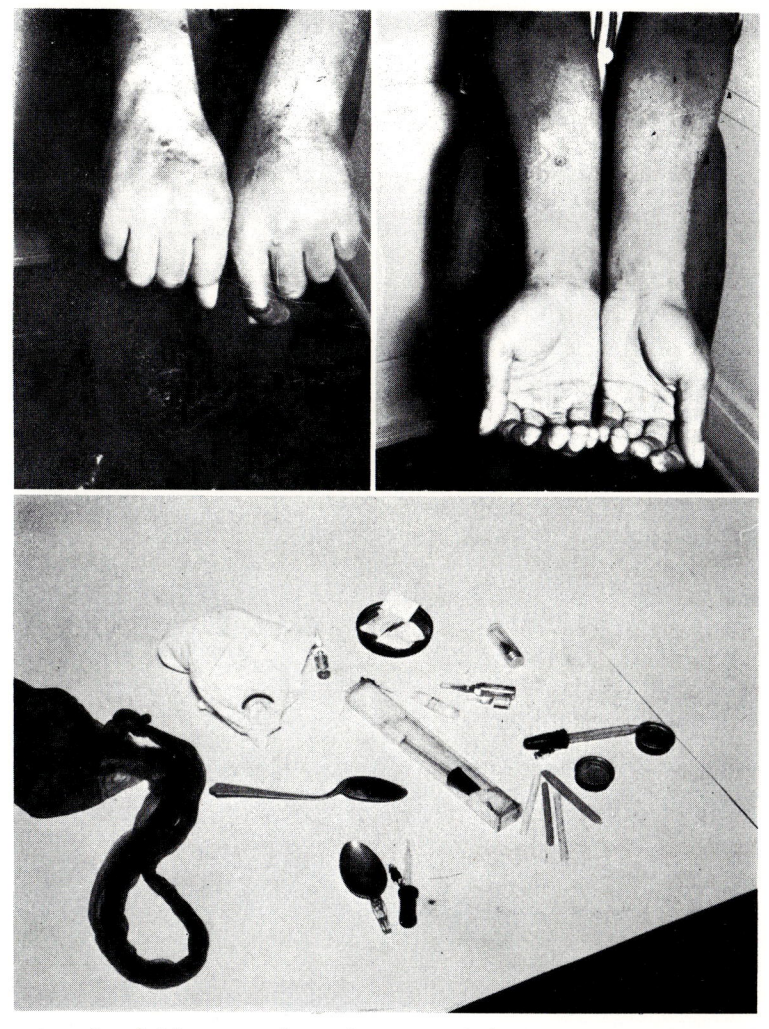

A series of welt-like scars along the veins of the arm are proof that he is on the "junk."

Anyone carrying an eyedropper with a hypodermic needle and a spoon or bottle cap, smoke blackened underneath, is an addict. He may, or may not, carry the narcotic, and a handkerchief or stocking to tie off the veins.

Retail drug stores and drug departments in department stores may be victims of shoplifters and possibly dishonest employes, but addicts pose an additional problem.

For the information of physicians and pharmacists who wish to protect themselves from inadvertently prescribing, administering or selling drugs to addicts, and for the information of law enforcement officers in the investigation of drug cases, several typical ruses used by addicts are presented:

7. An addict may secure a legitimate prescription for narcotics through one of the ruses described above, and purchase say, three dozen quarter-grain morphine tablets. Later he returns with the purchase, saying his doctor wants him to cut down the dosage and wants the druggist to exchange the quarter-grain tablets for eighth-grain tablets. However, the "quarter-grain tablets" he returns have been removed from the bottle and saccharin or other inert tablets substituted.[5]

14. A very common practice among addicts seeking medical narcotics is to obtain, usually by stealing, prescription blanks and forge a prescription for narcotics, complete with signature which they then present to a pharmacist for filling.[6]

Addicts are a peril to all retailers, of any commodities.

[1] Maurer, David W., Ph.D., Professor of English and the Humanities, University of Louisville, Lecturer on Narcotic Addiction and Criminal Argots, Southern Police Institute, Louisville, Kentucky; and Vogel, Victor H., M.D. Medical Officer in Charge, European Activities United States Public Health Service, Paris, France, formerly Medical Officer in Charge of United States Public Health Service Hospital, Lexington, Kentucky. *Narcotics and Narcotic Addiction,* Springfield, Illinois, Charles C Thomas, Publisher, Copyright 1954, p. 203.

[5] *Ibid.* p. 204-205.

[6] *Ibid.* p. 206.

Chapter 10
JUVENILE PROBLEMS OF STORES

"57 JUVENILES AMONG 72 ARRESTED AS WASHINGTON BIRTHDAY SHOPLIFTERS," headlines in a Washington, D.C. newspaper. Twenty-eight were boys and 29 were girls, most of them between 13 and 17 years of age.

Portland, Oregon, "CATCH 250 GIRLS AS SHOPLIFTING 'FAD' HITS TOWN. BOBBY SOCKS CRIME VICTIMIZES STORES." Police and juvenile court authorities confirmed a report of the Retail Trade Association that 150 to 175 girls of 12 to 15 years of age were detected shoplifting in a two months' period. The article indicated that shoplifting clubs were flourishing among school girls.

"UNCOVER TEEN-AGE SHOPLIFTING RING." Toledo, Ohio—A teen-age shoplifting and "refund" ring of 16 and 17-year-old girls fleeced the leading department stores by returning stolen merchandise for refunds. Two or three of the girls would operate as a unit and one would shoplift an item and give it to another member of the team. She would request a cash refund, stating the sales slip had been lost, then give a false name and address.

Similar articles have appeared in newspapers in many cities. Pilferage by juveniles is not confined to Washington, D.C., or Portland, or Toledo. The practice is probably typical for the entire country. **Juveniles form a large portion of all shoplifters.**

Data obtained from a study of records covering an eight-year period, 1943 through 1950, including 400 cases of boys and girls under 18 years of age, indicated that girls are more often, age for age, involved in the theft of valuable merchandise than boys.

More than 10 per cent of boys stole jewelry, billfolds, toys, books, and gadgets. More than 10 per cent of girls stole jewelry, billfolds, and dress accessories. Boys, more often than girls, take only one item of merchandise and less often steal more than five.

Girls were apprehended in peak numbers at about age 15, while the peak number of boys averages somewhat less than 15 years. Juvenile pilfering differs from adults in that it is more often done in groups. The proportion of pilferers, not professionals, "with others" at the time of arrest decreases with age. Juveniles are usually with one or more persons of the same sex and about the same age level. Boys ranged from none alone at 9 years of age to 100 per cent alone at 19 years. Girls ranged from none alone at 10 years of age to 85 per cent alone at 19 years.

A study of addresses of juvenile pilferers indicates that there is no relationship to slum areas. Proportionately as many come from prosperous neighborhoods and communities.

There was a decrease in juvenile pilferers during the World War II years, probably because many teen-agers had part time jobs or found odd jobs to keep them occupied. During the depression years of the 30's hardly a Saturday or a school holiday passed without one or more groups of children being apprehended. A noticeable change in the manners of teen-agers in the post-war years, is that they do not display the same superior attitude toward parents, as they generally displayed during the depression years.

There are times when store protection personnel can render a service to parents, by engaging a child in conversation, if he appears to be a truant. A comment, "you should be in school today, sonny," may be answered with an inadequate excuse that will pave the way for further questions and a telephone call might be made to the parent or the school.

When a sales person reported that a young boy had a roll of bills and was spending freely in the toy department on a school day, she was told to delay in wrapping the package. He was questioned and claimed that his school room had been excused for the day. A telephone call was made to the school and it was learned that the parents were looking for the boy because money had disappeared from the home.

A casual conversation once revealed that a boy was not only truant, but had also been away from home for several days, and another time a girl was discovered to be a run-away from home.

In the chapter on "Release or Prosecution" it is mentioned that most juveniles are released, after phoning the parents. Department stores in Chicago, in an effort to cooperate with the public officials in the juvenile delinquency program, are following a practice of notifying the police juvenile officer and following his instructions as to whether the arrested should be released or held for formal police and court action.

When apprehended, repeaters or professionals, children who may have run away from home, or those cases in which the interrogation, or the phone call, indicates negligence or delinquency of the parents, are sent to the juvenile officers of the police department.

Indications of professionalism are not common among juveniles. There have been several cases in which children have repeatedly attempted to return merchandise for cash refunds, for known adult shoplifters. Unless circumstances arise wherein the child can be detained and turned over to the police, the best procedure is to hold the merchandise and request that the sales check be brought in. If the merchandise has been stolen, there is usually no objection to leaving it, in fact the person often appears anxious to leave it and get away quickly.

If store personnel are trained to report all such cases, or suspicions, the protection department can eventually bring these cases to a conclusion; however, it is essential to use the utmost finesse in handling juveniles, just as it is with adults.

> The finesse with which defendant accosts plaintiff is a definite factor also affecting the temper with which the court approaches a case. The defendant acting in good faith with probable cause, whose attitude is quiet, non-threatening, and deferential to plaintiff's feelings can weather an honest mistake much more cheaply than otherwise. At the most it may induce a court to find there was no imprisonment at all. At the least, it will relieve defendant of punitive damages and reduce the amount of actual damages.[1]

[1] Inbau, Fred E., Professor of Law, Northwestern University, Protection and Recapture of Merchandise from Shoplifters, Reprinted by special permission of the *Illinois Law Review* (Northwestern University School of Law) Vol. 46, No. 6, 1952.

At one time I received a telephone call from the Captain of our district police station, informing me that a warrant had been issued for the arrest of one of my employes and myself. We went to the station where we were booked on a charge of false imprisonment, and posted bond.

The warrant had been obtained by a lawyer, a brother of a teen-age girl. The girl had not been imprisoned, nor detained against her wishes, and a "not guilty" verdict was rendered, even though the brother had negotiated a special prosecutor, a law school professor, for our trial.

Ample evidence had been accumulated to show justification for telling the girl that we would issue no further refunds to her. This was done with witnesses that she came to the protection department by herself, stood on the outside of a counter, was not touched nor detained in any way.

She had used a variety of names and addresses to obtain cash refunds on merchandise returned without sales checks. At times merchandise had been held and she was told, by the exchange clerk, to bring in the record of sale. No further claim would be made for the goods held. Instructions were given to personnel who recognized her, because of repeated visits, to direct her to the protection office when she again applied for a refund. This was intended as an indirect warning, but when she actually did arrive outside the office, she was told that no refunds would be made in the future, unless she presented the receipts with the merchandise. The records of a number of previous refunds or attempts to secure refunds were presented in our defense in the court.

Pickpockets are recognized by the underworld itself as professional criminals, even though they are classed as the lowest crooks on the underworld totem pole. One ten-year old black boy was apprehended in the act of picking a woman's purse. He was a "moll-buzzer" and proud of it; he even demonstrated his technique while awaiting the arrival of the juvenile officer.

The fact that he was somewhat small for his age probably assisted him. He was on an equal level with a purse carried over a woman's arm, and if he did jostle his victim, being a child, he might be excused without further investigation.

There are times when a shoplifting mother will be accompanied by children. Sometimes it is evident that the child will assist by taking or concealing the stolen article.

A twenty-two year old woman, who possessed a master's degree in biological sciences, was charged with teaching her sister, eleven, to steal.

A store detective had seen the two steal several articles of clothing and two books by putting them in a shopping bag. She followed them to a restroom where they emerged from a toilet booth wearing the stolen garments.

The younger girl, in court with their mother, at first insisted the thefts were her idea. Then she admitted to the judge that she had been told by her older sister to assume the blame on the theory that punishment for her would be less. The older girl was released on a $100 bond pending a psychiatric hearing and a motion for probation.

The most appalling episode of a small child being involved in professional crime came to my attention some years ago. A four-year old boy, in the company of his mother and her companion, was caught stealing an employe's purse from behind a counter. This climaxed a period of several years of purse thefts.

Boys, as well as men, have been caught prowling office desks of buyers, and stock areas, in search of purses.

The child, previously mentioned, started his career as a baby in arms. On several occasions we learned, while investigating the loss of employes' purses, that two women had sat in the section for a period of time and that one held a baby. Some time later we began to get reports of a toddler having been seen behind counters, before purses were discovered missing. Then we learned that a toddler had been seen taking a purse, and when the salesperson stopped him, the mother reprimanded him. Information was sent to other stores in the area and the two women and the boy were arrested while stealing a purse in one of the suburban stores.

"Hold Teen-Age Girls for Shoplifting," headlines to a story in a Chicago newspaper. We had arrested three girls, ages 14, 16, and 17, for the theft of wearing apparel. They were turned over to the police because of circumstances developed during interrogation. The 14-year-old had a parking check, for a car, in her purse. She had no driver's license, and we were doubtful that she was driving her father's car, as she stated. Investigation by the police found that the parked car had been stolen from in front of a suburban tavern. The 14-year-old admitted in the state's attorney's office that she had driven another stolen car earlier in the week.

Part time teen-age employes are a big help to retailers especially during peak business periods. Employment is also beneficial, economically, to the high school student. Merchants hiring youngsters owe them the duty of supervision and a set of rules designed to prevent temptation.

An investigation of cash losses eventually pointed to a 16-year-old boy, and when he was caught taking $10 he admitted the theft of $202 over a three months' period. Quoting, "I am sorry I took this money; I think the reason was, that I just could not resist the temptation."

One boy was stopped in an attempt to carry out a number of sweaters. He informed us that the idea for stealing developed after a conversation with another boy at a soft ball game. He had questioned the origin of the bat that was being used and was told that it had been stolen and also the method that was used in taking it out of the store. Quoting him, "The three times I took merchandise out, previous to last night, I took only one thing at a time. The reason was that the boy told me never to take a package which looked like more than I might buy. I had these sweaters 'planted' for quite some time and I can't explain what caused me to take them all last night."

In one instance a 44-year-old man was involved in thefts with two 16-year-old boys and one 17-year-old boy, all employes. We had information that one boy was selling "hot" merchandise. The information was given to the police who picked him up while he was making a sale. He involved the other two boys and the man, all of whom had been carrying merchandise out of the store on pass-outs authorized by a pass-out stamp which had been stolen from a desk. The stamp had not been reported missing.

Juvenile employes may not steal in groups, as pilferers do, but they do discuss their thefts among themselves.

Shortly after closing time one night a watchman saw a boy behind the camera counter. When questioned, the boy stated that he was looking for a half-dollar that had dropped there while he was flipping it. The watchman notified the door guard who observed the boy leaving the store at 7:40 p.m. and not carrying a package. The next morning we learned that the boy should have

Thefts of one teen-age, part-time employe.

left the store at 6:00 p.m., that the lock had been broken in a case where he had been seen and a $52.50 camera was missing. The boy was interrogated again and then he went to another floor and produced the stolen camera. He also admitted previously stealing a pair of $45 binoculars and other articles.

Nine days earlier a buyer had chased a boy from a sweater counter after closing time. The boy ran down an up-escalator and escaped. This boy was asked about the incident and while he denied being the boy who ran from the buyer, he identified the boy who had told him of the incident.

the animal nature of man, but compels them, changes them through a rational process which is called education.

Complexes are possible obstacles to the education and complexes may generate crime.

In reality what we teach children, adolescents, and young people is to dominate their instincts. Crime as a human fact is an episode of the fight for life which is in contrast with a social regulation having penal characteristics; it is an episode of the never ending fight for the acquisition of food and the female— of the battle which nature imposes on mankind.[2]

Retail stores are a source of temptation for working youths. Therefore, it is of the utmost importance for supervisors to realize that the education in prohibitions must continue outside the home and the school. It is necessary for stores to have controls aimed toward the prevention of delinquency of all employes. It is especially necessary for the supervisor of juveniles to be alert to his duty of enforcing the rules established to prevent delinquent behavior.

Chapter 11
NEIGHBORHOOD DEPARTMENT STORES

MORE professional shoplifters are arrested in neighborhood department stores than in downtown stores.

That is a statement of a young man, trained in protection work in a large store, who successfully reduced losses for two stores, annually doing approximately $1,000,000 each in sales.

At the time of his employment, by the operating company, two of their retail stores were suffering shrinkage of from 4 to 4.25 per cent. After dividing his time between two stores, for a period of six months, shrinkage dropped to approximately 2 per cent of sales. Another year of intensive work reduced shrinkage to about 1.5 per cent.

While the two stores were typical, and the volume of sales was comparable, there was a variance in neighborhoods. Shrinkage of one store located in a permanent neighborhood was reduced considerably under 1 per cent. The shrinkage of the other store, located in a transient neighborhood, remained slightly above 1 per cent at the lowest.

What caused the loss in these smaller stores? The factors contributing to loss or shrinkage were the same as in larger stores; shoplifters and pilferage by employes.

Store managers were reluctant to accept the suggestions that they were being victimized by professional thieves. The arrest of many shoplifters, with previous records, was proof that they were responsible for a substantial portion of the losses.

Shopping bags, booster skirts and bloomers, and all the equipment customarily used by boosters downtown, were found to be commonly used in the neighborhood stores.

An operator working on the selling floor of a smaller store finds it difficult to remain unknown to the public. "Plants" or hiding places for concealment contribute to the successful apprehension of thieves, in stores of limited size, even more so than in larger stores. They help to overcome the physical handicap of the layout, walls, fixtures, posts, and exits, that aid the thieves.

Two well dressed women participated in an episode in one of the stores. They entered the store and stopped to look at women's suits. One of them remained in the suit section and removed three of the most expensive suits from a wall case to a floor rack, while her companion went to another section and made a purchase.

The woman with the suits was well shielded, in a narrow aisle, by the rack on one side and a post opposite the spot she had selected to hang the suits. When the companion returned with her purchase and lifted the back of her skirt, the woman removed the three suits from the rack and quickly hooked the hangers to a belt worn by the companion under her dress. They were arrested as they left the store.

In another incident, two men entered the store. One stood just inside the entrance door, while the other one went to a nearby counter on which trousers were stacked. When the man at the door gave a nod, the one at the counter took an arm load of trousers and left the store.

The protection agent hurried to catch the thief but was blocked by the man standing at the door and had to push him aside. He was again interfered with by a third man who had waited outside the store and had to push him aside in order to run after the thief, who dropped the trousers.

All three men escaped but $700 worth of trousers were recovered.

This protection agent contends that the merchandise layout of the smaller stores dictates the loss pattern. The store manager transferred the trouser stock to the middle of the store but left leather jackets on a rack near the door.

A week later the same group of men returned. One man entered the store, grabbed an arm full of jackets from the rack and ran. This time there was no interference and the agent was able to overtake the thief who was knocked down and dropped the jackets. The thief gained his feet, drew a knife, and ran to an alley where he jumped on the rear bumper of a waiting car and again escaped. This time $500 worth of jackets were recovered.

The normal work force, of the two stores, totaled about eighty employes. Over a period of two and a half years about 40 employes, from stock boys to section managers, were apprehended stealing. Thefts ranged from a handkerchief to a $300 television set. Salespeople were "shopped" and some were found to be "knocking down" cash on sales.

Stock boys, who had the duty of disposing of waste, were discovered to be concealing merchandise in it. The articles were then picked up in the alley when the boys left for home.

Because of shortages in appliances, a unit control system was set up in the warehouse. When a $300 television set was unaccounted for, the records of the local trucking company hired to make deliveries were checked. They indicated a delivery of the missing set and the customer was interviewed to verify the purchase and delivery. Further investigation revealed the method used by the employe to steal the money paid by the customer.

The appliance salesman was assigned the duty of clearing the cash register at night. He had discovered that he could record his first cash sale of the day, pocket the proceeds, and then clear the register again. Every individual theft, even though well planned, is a risk. The safe system collapsed because, one day, the salesman's first transaction chanced to be the sale of an article that could be traced.

The most perplexing shrinkage was in a section tended, most of the time, by a saleslady who had been employed by the store for thirty years. She and her relievers had been shopped and the sales were properly recorded. Shoplifting and employe thefts were ruled out as a possibility for shrinkage. It was not unusual for a saleswoman, with that length of service, to have a personal clientele, but the fact that certain of her personal customers refused to purchase from relief salespeople was worth investigation.

The agent arranged a "plant" from which he could watch the cash register and wrapping desk; then he stayed away from the store for some time. By returning to the store while the suspected saleswoman was at lunch and immediately concealing himself, he was able to determine that the favored customers were purchasing one article and being given two.

Losses in these stores had been reduced, inventory results were satisfactory, and arrests had dwindled, so the protection agent was transferred to another branch of the business.

After the stores remained unprotected for a year, the shrinkage of one of the dress sections rose to 2.25 per cent. Four test inventories were taken at thirty day intervals, revealing a shrinkage of from $2,000 to $2,500 for each period. This indicated that over one hundred dresses were missing each month, as the highest priced garment was $22.95.

The agent returned to the store and the second day on the job solved the loss problem by arresting a group of professional boosters.

Three women, designated X, Y and Z, for the purpose of identifying their movements, entered the store. There was no immediate indication that the three were together but they all went to the dress section.

X looked at dresses staying within a limited area. Y and Z roamed throughout the section, selecting dresses of various sizes and styles, which they would hang on a rack near X. Dresses were being assembled to be stolen.

When they were ready to boost, Y stood on one side of X and held up a dress as a shield. Z had come close to X on the other side and quickly slipped dresses under her coat that X removed from the rack, folded and handed to her; Z and Y then shifted positions and X again removed dresses from the rack, quickly rolled them around the hangers, and handed them to Y who put them under her coat.

X remained in the section, again examining dresses, while Z walked in one direction and Y in another. They both stopped, looked around, walked further, hesitated, and then left the store by different exits.

Y and Z soon returned to the store and the same maneuvers were repeated, when Y and Z left with dresses, X again remained in the store and this time the store manager had been alerted to watch her while the agent and another store employe went outside.

Y and Z went to a parked car, with a man in the driver's seat, and entered the back seat. The agent opened both the front and rear doors of the car, informed the occupants that they were under arrest, and waited for a police squad he had summoned from the district station.

Y and Z were found to have pillow cases pinned inside their coats in which the dresses were deposited. Dresses valued at more than $200 were in their possession, on their persons and in the car. Almost $800 worth of women's and children's apparel, from other stores, was found in the trunk of the car.

When her companions did not return to the store X left, but while she waited, she had assembled a number of skirts that probably would have gone had Y and Z made another trip.

This incident occurred at about the half way point of a monthly inventory which was short about $800. Shrinkage the following month was $10 and for the next three month period it was approximately $100.

The agent is now managing the protection department of one of the downtown stores. He states that according to his experience in the neighborhoods, most shoplifting occurred there on days, and at the time of day, when there was just enough traffic to keep salespeople busy, with few customers standing around and watching.

Full time protection may not be a necessity for the smaller stores. It is advisable to have all supervisory personnel alerted to the problems that may be encountered and trained in loss prevention.

Any company operating a chain of retail outlets will find a well organized and experienced protection department an asset. Test inventories should be taken during the fiscal year to determine when, where, and how much protection is necessary in various stores.

A store does not need to be big in order to require protection.

Chapter 12
CANDY—FOODS—SELF-SERVICE MARKETS

SELLING price and cost accounting methods are both used in operating food sections. The retail method is often used by selling sections of department stores, and the cost method by food processing rooms and restaurants. Either way, it is advisable to maintain effectual controls in order to reduce shrinkage results for the retail sections, and to show a satisfactory profit for the cost operated department.

The transfer of foods from a workroom to a selling section can be easily controlled by unit or weight counts. Most foods that are served to be eaten on the premises are regulated by the unit or the size of the utensil used in serving, or by the container from which the food is served. The quantity of meat being served or used in sandwiches is often determined by weight.

The loss of profit in cost accounting sections may be due to the actions of employes; therefore security controls should apply to workers behind the scenes, as well as food check regulations for the waiters or salespeople.

Servers who record food or drink sales on cash registers have been apprehended stealing money. Honesty shopping is advisable.

Kitchen workers have been caught stealing cold meats, butter, coffee, other foods, linens, and utensils, by carrying them on their person or by walking out with shopping bags full.

Locker or dressing rooms should be located away from production areas and arranged so that supervisors can observe articles carried in and out of them. A system for checking goods received and security for the receiving room is important.

The enforcement of package pass-out procedures are just as important for food workers as for all other employes. One employe who was given bones to take home added meat to the package. A butcher ordered a duck from a vendor and when it was delivered he added steaks to the package. He had readily obtained a pass-out on the duck, an item which was not currently stocked.

A definite procedure should be established for the disposal of left over or discarded foods. If left over items are made available for the use of night maintenance workers, arrangements should be made to have it picked up before the kitchen or pantry supervisor leaves. It should be carried away with an itemized and signed authorization. The giving away of foods can be of benefit to some employes, but it can also be detrimental to an operation. Employes who have been given left-overs have been caught pilfering in kitchens when the left-over quantities received were insufficient.

Even the salvaging of scraps from garbage can be a hazard. One maintenance man, who had been given permission to salvage food for his dogs, was caught stealing roasts which he concealed with the scraps.

Because many people do not consider that taking food in small quantities is stealing, employes can create problems for food sections after regular store hours. Signs, to be placed on candy and other food counters at closing time, may prevent temptation for some workers, if they read "Sampling Of Foods Is Considered Stealing."

While the food filcher may not consider his acts a theft, other persons may steal food in quantities. A closet was watched because a carton of nuts, open with some of the contents missing, was found hidden in it. When an employe was apprehended, removing nuts from the carton, he admitted the theft of many articles besides foods and nuts.

Food sections operating on the selling price accounting basis have shrinkage problems in addition to shoplifting and pilferage.

If samples of foods, especially candy, are furnished to prospective customers, markdowns should be taken to adjust the shrinkage. This can be done by setting aside samples in quantities, or on a percentage to sales basis if samples are taken from stock. Also some manufacturers will supply a quantity for samples.

All employes handling breakable merchandise should be instructed in the proper markdown procedure for damaged articles, and it is especially important that food salespeople be so trained. Foods are vulnerable to spoilage and breakage.

loss prevention measures and approved apprehension techniques; secondly, personnel of the security department are sent into stores to watch for shoplifters; also the shopping, checking, and investigations of employes suspected of stealing are supervised by the department. Finally, the fact that all professional shoplifters apprehended are prosecuted soon becomes general knowledge among thieves and acts as a restraining factor.

There are approximately 27,000 self-service food supermarkets in the United States while there are some 310,000 grocery outlets. The spacious parking lots of the supermarkets are an aid to those thieves who visit a number of locations in one day and attempt to beat the check out system.

Shrinkage of one kind has been largely eliminated, for some self-service markets, by the sharply stepped up use of transparent, visual, packaging materials. Fresh fruits and vegetables, once purchased by the shopper on a pinch-and-squeeze basis which caused great loss, are rapidly being prepackaged and price marked. It is reported that spoilage loss has been cut as much as fifty per cent.

Security departments have proven effective in reducing loss and shrinkage for some of the midwestern Food Chains by combatting the type of self-service without payment.

The manager of security, for one chain of some 200 stores, has determined that the training of store managers in loss prevention measures and the techniques of apprehension is the answer to some of his problems. An exchange of information is conducted with all stores covering any current problems.

The exchange of information pays off because loss patterns unfold for self-service stores the same as for department stores. Several store managers reported similar actions of a customer to the central office. Notices to alert all store managers were sent out. They gave a description of a man and his method of operation.

He would approach the checker with a cart full of groceries, then explain that he would have to go to his wife, who was in his car, to get more money. He would carry a package out with him and then fail to return. Within a few days he was arrested by a store manager. He had five cartons of stolen cigarettes in the bag he carried out. He was a narcotic addict.

The three items most commonly stolen from self service stores by professional thieves are cigarettes, canned hams, and cosmetics or toilet goods.

One woman professional shoplifter, a crotch worker, was apprehended carrying six cartons of cigarettes between her thighs. Upon investigation it was discovered that another woman, who was arrested, was carrying twenty cartons of cigarettes tucked between three girdles that she was wearing.

One of the first acts of a protection manager, who had recently assumed charge of a large company, was to install a system for each store to apply their identification stamp on each carton of cigarettes. This enabled him to effect the arrest of a clever thief.

When an acquaintance remarked that his wife could buy cigarettes for a reduced price, from a woman who canvassed taking orders for various kinds of merchandise, the company man requested a purchase. It proved to be from one of his outlying stores.

After the seller was identified, the security man spent one morning trailing the thief. He was in the vicinity of her home when she left and her one half day's work left her temporarily in possession of over $200 worth of stolen merchandise from four stores, in addition to stolen cigarettes from two self-service stores.

On two trips to her car, from one store, the woman had four children's dresses, a snow suit, and a pair of pants. At another store she made two trips to her car with a girl's coat, a sweater, a pair of jeans, and a skirt. She got three pairs of pants and a suede jacket at her third stop, and five sheets at another one. All the merchandise was carried between her thighs to the car. She also stole the cigarettes from two markets and upon arrest she voluntarily turned over to the police a quantity of previously stolen merchandise she had in her home.

The woman, a wife and a mother of three children, had supplemented her husband's moderate income and had purchased a $35,000 home with a two car garage which she had filled with current year automobiles. She did well before she was caught, due to a casual conversation.

One couple, a man and a woman with a child in a stroller, were arrested at one of the markets after they had by-passed the checking counter. They left the store with $6.50 worth of meats and groceries, but their car contained $150 worth of stolen goods.

Shoplifting and Shrinkage Protection

The items were from department stores as well as groceries from another supermarket. There were twenty boxes of hose, two house dresses, toys and miscellaneous articles.

Three young women and a male driver of their car, all narcotic addicts, were caught with quantities of nylon hose, cigarettes, and canned hams.

An eighty year old man, who was caught hiding about two dollars worth of merchandise in his pockets, confessed that he had stolen food every day for years. His alibi was that his old age pension was insufficient for him to live on.

A period of unemployment, in any one area, is probably responsible for some increase in shoplifting in food stores. After a few months of increased unemployment the protection personnel of food-chains report some increase in both shoplifting and bad checks.

Parking lots are a hazard for the supermarkets. It is not unusual to find merchandise valued at hundreds of dollars in the cars of professional thieves. Stores in transient areas are also likely to suffer losses. As a result, some stores need closer surveillance and more often. Where it is indicated that a particular store is having inventory shortages, the services of the security men should be requested by the manager, superintendent, or district manager in charge of that particular store. If it appears that the public is responsible for losses, the store employes can be given specific training to be on guard.

The statement has been made that more store managers loose their jobs because of inventory shrinkage than for any other reason. That alone should cause every store manager to take advantage of all the services offered by the central security office.

Some stores have built elaborate "plants" where a watcher can be concealed. In the Chicago area, "peep holes" in existing partitions are sometimes used to spot shoplifters in self-service stores. Other methods of apprehension are to take a concealed position where the customers' actions and movements can be observed or to pose as a shopper so that customers can be watched more closely.

The failure of cashiers to turn the key and lock cash register drawers, when they left a check out counter, gave "till-tappers" an opportunity to hit one chain twice in a week. Two young men, one short and one tall, worked together. While the short one kept a cashier busy in one aisle, the tall one rifled a cash drawer in an adjoining aisle.

Employe thefts are also a problem to the security personnel of food stores. Cashier checkers have found ways to pocket money. One method is to fail to record an expensive item on the register, then to add it on the tape in pencil after checking the items against the list. These thefts can be uncovered by shopping for honesty.

In one week, one store manager, two market managers and a helper admitted thefts of $15,000 from one chain. Polygraph tests were given during the investigation to assist in determining the total loss.

The protection manager for another chain of food stores was plagued by a series of cash shortages in a new store. About the time they had reached $1,500 he was given a tip, on the cause, by a detective from a department store branch which was located in the same shopping center.

A cashier in the self-service store had stolen merchandise from the department store. She had been apprehended there because her husband would return it, without sales checks, for cash refunds. She was released by the food store and the cash shortages stopped.

Independently owned self-service groceries and markets, associated with a chain group for merchandising and supervision, operate under the retail accounting method. An average percentage is recommended for inventory shrinkage.

The owner of one of these stores checks his shelves every morning, when he opens, to find evidence of thefts. Evidence usually consists of empty boxes and cartons that have contained luncheon meat, aspirin, tooth paste, gauze, etc.; or it may be one or two eggs missing from a carton. The items that are stolen without leaving evidence are never known.

This owner follows the practice, when he sees anyone attempting to steal an article, of telling them to put it on the counter.

The same market had cashed bad checks for more than $900 in one year. After installing an identifying camera only one loss has been suffered. The one was a government check stolen from the mail and cashed by a female narcotic addict who was wanted by a number of stores. A good photographic likeness of her was obtained, also pictures of the check and the identification used. It is ironical to note that the identification carried the notation, "not to be used as identification." The assistant manager, who cashed the check, saw a sale of a cart of groceries and did not read the card he accepted as identification.

Records of Food Chains indicate that the most common offender is the housewife. Her first theft is usually an item such as a quarter pound of butter, or a small can of tuna, or something that is easily concealed in a purse or pocket. She graduates to more and larger items and if she steals a quantity of merchandise, or is a repeater, they have no choice but to prosecute.

Only about two per cent of the non-professional shoplifters taken into custody indicate that a desperate need for financial assistance was the reason for stealing.

Over 4,000 shoplifters have been arrested in one chain in four years. Of this number, 890 were considered to be professional thieves, many of them drug addicts.

One company that has made a concerted effort to combat crime in their markets is the Acme Markets-American Stores. The Public Safety Department, in cooperation with the Philadelphia, Pennsylvania, Police Department, has issued a pamphlet, *Shoplifter Racket Tricks of the Trade*, aimed at reducing Supermarket thefts.

Candy stores, groceries, bakeries, supermarkets, all face the same loss hazard that confronts all retail establishments. Shoplifting, employe thieving, confidence game and bad check artists, burglaries and hold-ups, all are essential reasons for such stores to maintain a security and loss prevention program.

Chapter 13

FRAUDULENT CHECKS—CHARGES— CONFIDENCE GAME

THERE is no decisive formula enabling store personnel to spot fraudulent bank checks and charge take-with-purchases. However, every confidence perpetrator will commit some act that will cause someone to become suspicious. Some people will never sense a wrong, while others, having a discriminating power of cognition, will recognize these attempts of "false pretense," or "confidence game."

Store personnel, having the responsibility for authorizing bank checks and charge take transactions, should be instructed in the action to be taken in case of suspicion.

Advice from *Forgery and Fictitious Checks:*

> The first thought to be kept in mind is that the money in the cash register is either your property or the property of the firm which employs you; it is therefore your responsibility to establish the validity of the check or order, and then to establish the identity of the presenter or endorser of the check or order. Particular caution should be exercised by all persons who in their course of employment in any place of business have to place their O.K. on checks or orders when they are presented on the floor in payment for merchandise.[1]

In Illinois—

> A person who uses false pretenses in order to cheat or defraud someone of money or property is guilty of the misdemeanor generally called by the appropriate name of "false pretenses." (a) The case illustration given in the previous section of false impersonation to obtain merchandise would also constitute false pretenses, because of the pretense of being another person; however, under the latter charge the offense would be

---

[1] Sternitzky, Julius L.: *Forgery and Fictitious Checks,* Charles C Thomas, Publisher, Springfield, Illinois, 1955, p. 63-64.

punishable as a misdemeanor, whereas under the false impersonation charge it would be the felony of larceny. Nevertheless, there is one unique and practically advantageous feature of the false pretense statute—a provision in it to the effect that in addition to being subject to a fine and imprisonment the convicted person "shall be sentenced to restore the property so fraudulently obtained, if it can be restored."

Another pertinent illustration of the commission of this offense of false pretenses is the obtaining of credit or the opening of a charge account by means of intentionally making false statements in writing regarding responsibility or means or ability to pay. (b)

Another relevant misdemeanor closely related to the crime of false pretenses is that of fraudulently cashing a check where there is either no account or insufficient funds in the bank upon which the check is drawn; but before one is guilty of this offense it must be established that he cashed the check "with intent to defraud"; and an innocent mistake is a complete defense to any such charge. (c)

Confidence Game. The crime of obtaining money or property by means of a confidence game is actually nothing more than the employment of false pretenses coupled with the winning of the confidence of the victim in the offender as an individual. In other words, to be guilty of using a confidence game the offender in effect must "sell himself" to the victim; he seeks to and does gain the victim's good will, confidence, and trust, rather than just lie about some incidental matter such as his identity or the contents of a box or something of that sort.

Because of this confidential element, this crime carries with it a greater penalty than does false pretenses alone.(d)[2]

"Bad" checks come in various forms. Government checks, good on the face, might be bad on the back if the endorsement is forged; dividend and other types of checks the same. It is not unusual for these checks to be stolen from mail boxes along with other mail.

[2] Inbau, Fred E., Professor of Law, Northwestern University, Manual for Store Protection, prepared for and published by The Retail Special Service Association, Inc., 1951, p. 32-33.
    a. Section 253 *Illinois Criminal Code.*
    b. Section 254 *Illinois Criminal Code.*
    c. Section 255 *Illinois Criminal Code.*
    d. Section 256 to 259 *Illinois Criminal Code.*

Postal employes have also been apprehended stealing mail. Therefore envelopes are not satisfactory identification.

Forged government checks are investigated by the United States Secret Service, a part of the Treasury Department. However, such action does not necessarily recover the loss suffered by a merchant who cashes the checks. The Secret Service has conducted a nationwide campaign, "Know Your Endorser," designed to prevent the theft and forgery of checks.

Another kind of check crook is one who prints, or has printed, checks bearing the name of some well known company. The spurious checks will be executed with a typewriter and check protector and may appear to be genuine, although some are so poorly imitated it is surprising that the forger is successful in cashing them. Checks have been cashed with the name of a large company rubber stamped on the check. Bogus identification is usually used in cashing fraudulent checks.

Publicity of an arrest, "Ex-Convict, 78 Held As Tutor of Check Gang," stated that Federal Bureau of Investigation agents who arrested him accused him of tutoring members of a $100,000 counterfeit check and stolen money order ring. The 78 year old man had a 57 year police record. Members of the gang were arrested in Los Angeles and Chicago.

Blocks of blank money orders have been stolen in burglaries and cashed. At other times "no account," "not sufficient funds," "account closed," or "forged signature" checks are presented on a purchase, or for cashing.

The majority of fraudulent passers are caught sometime, prosecuted, and convicted. There is an extensive exchange of information on bad checks in Chicago. Police, Government Agencies, banks, currency exchanges, hotels, and stores, all get information and are on the alert as soon as information is received. Many of the people apprehended have previously served time for the offense.

Various protective methods have been devised to assist the smaller stores and shops to reduce their check losses. A method of thumb printing with a colorless creme is in use, and a camera that simultaneously photographs the person who presents the check, the check itself, and the identification presented is also being used.

In stores where checks are accepted in the selling areas, for merchandise purchased, the personnel must be educated to the "danger signals." The bad check passer may talk too much or he may talk too little. Like the shoplifter, his actions are frequently different from those of the honest customer.

Any seeming delay in delivering the merchandise or change on a bad check may cause a crook to leave suddenly, but the best protection against check or fraudulent purchase losses is alertness of employes.

On a Saturday afternoon a chic young woman selected some $30 worth of merchandise and presented a personal check drawn on an eastern bank. Her identification was apparently good and there was no reason for the authorizer to doubt her check; however he did watch as she left the counter. She walked to an exit and handed the package she had just purchased to a man who was standing there and holding several other packages.

When the woman walked to another counter and started to make a selection, the authorizer phoned the protection department. On completion of her selection, she again presented a check drawn on the same bank. Arrangements had been made between the detective and the authorizer to approve the check.

The detective followed the two when they left the store and the woman entered one hotel and the man went to another one.

On Monday morning a telephone call was put through to the eastern bank and it developed that a woman and two men were wanted in various parts of the country for cashing thousands of dollars worth of "no account" checks. They had defrauded stores, hotels, air lines, etc.

City detectives were notified and they were able to locate the three people in the two hotels. Easy living ended for the three, not because of any awareness of the bad checks, but because a store employe acted on a "hunch." F.B.I. agents entered the case and the trio was convicted and sentenced.

Another employe, who had studied the mannerisms of "customers" who appear too glib with answers and too fast with excuses, prevented a fraudulent charge and assisted in the recovery of

Fraudulent Checks—Charges—Confidence Game

money paid out on forged checks and the apprehension of three robbers.

The manner in which a young man selected two expensive cigarette cases, and his urgency for speed, caused a salesman to be suspicious when a credit plate was presented. The salesman suggested that they save time by going to the credit office to have the transaction approved. Immediately the customer requested the salesman to go to the office while he went to meet a friend "waiting outside." The diplomacy of the salesman proved him to be a better "con-man" than the customer. "It'll only take a moment and you'll be less delayed if we go up right now together." So they went to the credit office and, because the customer became more nervous, protection was called.

The young man had a wallet full of excellent identification but he was unable to answer questions concerning data of a personal nature found among the various papers. His "mother," the customer to whom the account belonged, was called and the suspect was put on the wire. He put up a good bluff but it is hard to fool a mother about her son's voice.

The real son was called and he asked to have the man detained for the police who were in his apartment at the time. Our customer and two accomplices had been in the real son's apartment, tied him up, ransacked the apartment of clothing, luggage, etc., stolen the charge plate and come to our store. They had used the plate to cash two checks before one of them attempted to purchase the two expensive cigarette cases. The two accomplices were also arrested by the police.

When a youth selected two expensive ties and two expensive handkerchiefs, and then presented a credit plate, the saleswoman asked if Mrs. ——— was his mother. "No," replied the boy, "she's my aunt." The salesperson asked the boy to wait a moment; then she called the credit office. A phone call was made to the customer, who found her plate missing from her purse. The aunt came to the store and it was discovered that her nephew had used her plate to make a number of purchases.

Another different fraudulent purchases case made the news:

"She Needs $1,000. Buys Way Into Jail; Can't Buy Way Out."
"A blond from Kansas City was in a County Jail cell today, trying to raise $1,000, needed to make bail." "A Whee of a Shopping Spree," "$125.69 Will Get You Mink, Rings, Clothes and the Police!"

The woman, who said that she had a little fuss with her husband and had come to Chicago, carried a screw driver in her purse, and a wrench, pliers, and a knife in a railroad station locker. She claimed they belonged to her husband and she just happened to have them around.

Somehow perhaps with the use of her tools, the woman had acquired the charge account credentials along with a check for $125.69, the property of a Greater Chicago citizen. She proceeded to purchase a $600 mink scarf, some dresses, earrings, blouses, a brooch, and a man's suit. While the credit rating of the account was good, this was an unusual amount of activity for one day, and credit authorizers are paid a reward for discovering the use of stolen credentials.

A phone call was made to the real Mrs. ——— who said that she had lost her charge plate and had not been in the store that day. Soon another call requesting authorization for the purchase of a $698 diamond ring was made, but the police were waiting. When approached, the woman popped the ring into her mouth but was forced to spit it out. "I just got foolish,"-she said in explanation.

The removal of incriminating evidence from upon or within the body of accused persons is covered by:

> ". . . The court reasoned that if the defendant had concealed the rings in his hands or placed them in his mouth the police would have had a legal right to forcibly open his hand or mouth; therefore, they had a right to resort to the enema process, for if the act of the officers should be considered unusual, it was brought on by reason of the act of the accused party.[3]

Store personnel can spot some "false impersonators" without

---

[3] Inbau, Fred E.: *Self Incrimination*, Charles C Thomas, Publisher, Springfield, Illinois, 1950, p. 71-72.

prior knowledge of a certain account being used. However, the greatest success in arresting persons misrepresenting themselves as charge customers has been due to dilligent work of protection personnel and the co-operation of salespeople.

As soon as a notice of fraudulent charges is received, either from a customer or the credit authorization division, an investigation is made to determine the description of the impersonator and the kind of articles being purchased.

All pertinent information is distributed to salespeople. If the impersonator is not caught quickly, protection personnel will tour the store and give a personal reminder to all employes.

An excellent description of one person was received from a saleswoman. Vitamins, worth $14, were purchased one day and two days later the same person purchased $6 worth from another salesperson. This caused the one employe to observe the customer closely. After an investigation was made, the salesperson thought about it from time to time with a feeling that the customer would return. Sure enough it happened! While busy with another sale— "out of the corner of my eye I saw the woman; then I asked a fellow employe to call protection, and I finished with my customer. I left the counter, followed the woman to another section, watched her make a purchase and leave that counter. I told another employe to watch for the detective and tell him the direction I was taking. Along the way I gave the same information to another employe and when the woman started to make a purchase in another section, two detectives were there to take charge."

A mighty pretty and exclusive coat was the reason another young "customer" was caught. A description of the coat was delivered to salespeople and when the young lady strolled into the store the following day it was recognized. The woman who had sold the coat was called to identify it and the wearer. The employe immediately informed the section manager, who instructed another saleslady to watch while a phone call was made to protection.

Within a matter of minutes, detectives arrived and asked the young woman to accompany them to their headquarters. Then the woman began to talk. She knew the customer and her daughter had a charge account at the store—why not represent herself as the daughter and sign her name to the charge slip? "I wonder where I slipped up?" mused the girl in the new coat.

The customer and her daughter had received a bill. The coat, of course, was not on that charge bill—it had been purchased only the day before—but there were other items on the bill that the customer had not purchased; therefore, she and her daughter immediately visited the store with a complaint.

Another incident which shows what top teamwork can accomplish: A woman said, "I'll take this jacket and these two sweaters—here's my charge plate."

The salesperson glanced at the little plate, but remained calm, and while wrapping the purchase, whispered to another salesperson who walked around the counter and talked to the section manager. The calm presence of mind of the salesperson, the equally calm but quick action of the fellow worker and the manager, and the speed with which the detective arrived on the scene cleared up another problem. Nine hundred dollars worth of merchandise had been fraudulently purchased.

"Kiting" checks is another kind of "Confidence Game." Kiting is the keeping up a bank balance by writing and cashing checks in order to make bank deposits. The scheme is usually worked to overcome a temporary shortage of funds, but it can become so involved that it suddenly collapses and stores are sometimes left holding "not sufficient funds" checks. An investigation should be made if one customer is known to be cashing checks in substantial amounts every day.

In one such case that collapsed, a woman confessed to the State's Attorney that she had kited checks for $165,000 to help her husband's failing business. Despite all the kiting, the total losses to stores and business houses totaled only about $15,000.

A victim for a short-con racket, commonly called "pigeon-drop," is occasionally singled out of shoppers in department and variety stores. In this racket, often participated in by women, the victim selected will be an elderly woman. After one has started a conversation with the victim, a confederate will pass by and drop an envelope or package. Upon examination, the con-woman will find a sum of money in it and will then suggest that the victim hold it until the owner is found. But in order to prove good faith, the victim must put up a sum of money. At times the victim may go to a bank and draw out a sum of money, sometimes in the thousands. In exchange for this, she will receive a package of paper which has been substituted for the one containing the money.

While the "games" may start in a store, they are usually concluded at another location. Alert store detectives have recognized the actions and notified city police who follow through.

Another wretched "petty-con" was worked on young service men, during the war, and is still successful with some young men who seem to be strangers in a city. The con-man will spot his victim near a railroad station and start a conversation. The conversation will turn to a baseball or football game, a theater play, or some other event, and the suggestion will be made that the young man attend. When they approach a department store, the stranger will suggest that the young man purchase a ticket, which is hard to obtain. Then the con-man will take the victim's money and instruct him to wait at an entrance, while he himself goes to a ticket sales area in the store where he has an "in." When the victim becomes tired of waiting, he talks to a store employe and then finds his way to the protection department.

Store personnel should know that possession of counterfeit money is no crime unless the possessor has the knowledge that it is counterfeit and intends to use it to defraud.

> Because of the extreme difficulty in determining whether a person who has passed or attempted to pass counterfeit money is aware of the fact that it is counterfeit, the protection agent should ordinarily not make an arrest in such cases. All he can safely do is to try to obtain, without involuntary detention, the name and address of the individual and notify the Secret Service as quickly as possible. The counterfeit money, itself, should be retained by the store once it has come into the hands of a cashier or salesperson.[4]

[4] Inbau, Fred E., Professor of Law, Northwestern University, *Manual for Store Protection,* prepared for and published by The Retail Special Service Association, Inc. 1951, p. 37.

Acts of embezzlement by employes are committed against their employers in all types of business. Stores are no exception.

The protection department of a large store will be challenged by almost every known type of Fraud or Con-game.

Attempts have been made to "borrow" money from executives and their secretaries, by professional con-artists. Women and children have made a racket of begging carfare from store employes, by using a hard luck tale. Men have been intimidated by chance acquaintances, met in washrooms, who pose as police officers.

Store employes can often prevent loss by being alert to the smooth, fast talking stranger who schemes to defraud by a confidence game.

Chapter 14
HONESTY SHOPPING

THE PRESIDENT of one of the first organized shopping services stated that back in 1915 after shopping a drug store, one of a chain whose stock shortages were running about 5 per cent, the shoppers reported that a young salesman was putting the money from each sale in his pocket.

The interview:

"What made you feel that it would be all right for you to steal?" "Well," he answered, "I handle money all day. One day I needed money for lunch, so I took it. I intended to pay it back but I never got around to it. I learned that it is easy to steal."

"You must have felt confident that you would not be detected. What made you feel so confident?"

He replied, "Although I handle money and the cash register all day, no one ever pays any attention to me. I work with the cash drawer open all day. I don't put ink on the cash register tape. Sometimes I don't even put any tape in the register."

"You mean to tell me that the store manager does not supervise your activities?"

"That is right," he answered. "If the manager of the store had cautioned me about errors which I make or if he had corrected me when I violated store rules or policies, I wouldn't have taken the chances which I have taken. I would have been afraid that he would take some action if he again found me violating company rules. He never checked up on me and I began to feel that there was no risk involved in stealing from the company. That's why I started to steal. I have been doing it for a long time, until you people came in and caught me."[1]

---

[1] Bernstein, Mark, President, Willmark Service System, Inc., New York. *Preventing Losses Due to Employe Pilferage.* p. 2. Clinic on Shoplifting and Other Store Protection Problems, conducted by Chicago Retail Merchants Association, Illinois Federation of Retail Associations, in cooperation with Associated Food Retailers of Greater Chicago; Chicago Paint and Wallpaper Association; Chicago Retail Druggists Association; Chicago Retail Hardware Association; Jewelers Association of Greater Chicago; The Retail Special Service Association, Inc. March 10, 1954.

Testing for honesty is important, almost imperative, for the smaller shop as well as for larger stores. There is the same need for honesty shopping today as there was in 1915. Shopping services may be secured from a shopping service organization, by employe shoppers, or by a system of rewards to customers. Some restaurants and shops display a sign advising patrons to watch the cash register check for a red symbol, which, if received, will pay the customer a cash reward. Other small shops may display a sign requesting customers to wait for their register receipt. A sticker applied to the cash register, stating that the store is serviced by a shopping service, may act as a deterent to employes tempted to pocket money.

It is just as important for the customer to have the sales receipt, either register or book check, as it is for the sale to be recorded.

A dishonest employe may fail to record a sale and pocket the proceeds, or he may record the sale and retain the record of sale, which may later be given to another customer and the money kept, or used to ship merchandise out, or used as a pass-out.

Two store detectives observed one young man make a sale for $5.81. The merchandise was wrapped and handed to the customer without being recorded. The young man walked to the cash register, stood there, looked around, and then, as he approached another customer, he slipped the money into his pocket. He admitted having stolen money previously in the same manner. He had taken money from about ten sales that day and had only recorded $2.17 on his cash register.

On the following day, in another part of the store, a salesman was observed to make a sale totaling $5.97. After giving the merchandise to the customer, he loitered near the cash register for a while, and then walked over to a cashier; after he got some change, he returned to the register, played with the keys, glanced around, walked to another counter, and put the money in his coat pocket.

One employe was greatly relieved when shopping indicated that she had been "knocking down" on sales, and she readily admitted that she had stolen about $2,000. Her reason was that her husband, who gambled on the races, demanded money of her regularly. She claimed that once she started stealing she did not have the will power to stop.

At times, some action of an employe will cause someone, a fellow worker, a supervisor, or a detective, to become suspicious of him. Customers sometimes question the lack of a sales receipt or report some apparent irregularity of a salesperson. In case of suspicion the employe should be shopped, and not only once, but often enough to assure that money is being turned in properly.

Some employes will "knock down" or pocket the full amount of a sale, while others will only take part of it, possibly $1 at a time. Still another one will perhaps take $4 or $10. One may steal just prior to a payday, while another may do so regularly, at every opportunity.

Early in my career, one salesperson was reported as under suspicion. She was shopped several times and even though the shopper walked away without waiting for a sales receipt, the money was recorded properly. She was again reported and again she was shopped until we felt that the reports were unfounded.

Some six months later, on a routine shopping, not a special request, it was found that she had not recorded a $5 sale. She confessed to having taken some $600 over a period of several years, the entire amount at only $5 at a time, no more, no less.

In this case the shopper remembered while passing the counter that she had been requested to shop the salesperson at one time. This time she just happened to purchase the right amount at the right time to clear up the case.

There are other good reasons for shopping employes. Any salesperson known to be gambling regularly or living beyond apparent means is a good prospect.

A letter signed "Sincerely Yours, A Mother," gave a lead at one time. She requested us to have "these dens," meaning bookies, closed. She had a problem and so did we; however she gave the address of a bookie and we assumed that we apprehended her daughter, after shopping an employe who frequented this "bookie."

I am a widow and have quite a problem. It is my daughter who has been gambling with your money. She promised me *faithfully that she would not gamble. Today I followed her on her lunch hour and she went to _____ and made an $8 wager. Not to create a scene I had to keep still. . . .*

Another tip came from a section manager. He reported that a saleswoman, in his department, had purchased a $600 wedding dress for her daughter, much more than he had paid for his daughter's wedding dress. He also reported that there had been a large hotel reception which he knew she could not afford. She was shopped and found to be stealing money from sales.

An employe suspected of stealing merchandise might also be shopped. Some may steal goods but never think of taking money. Others will take both.

One employe was apprehended when he used a salescheck to send out an article for $295 on an even exchange basis, with a forged authorizing signature. In addition to stealing merchandise, he admitted stealing money from sales. He was not caught because of shopping, but he might have been, because of failure to give the shopper a copy of the salescheck.

Quoting some of his remarks:

There are loopholes in the system that are obvious to anyone who has studied economics. You can steal a book of saleschecks as I did, then take the saleschecks out of the stolen salesbook, write up a salescheck for a piece of merchandise worthwhile and send it out to a rented room or hotel room. You would not need to turn in the original book check. The only way they would ever catch up with you would be for the delivery man to become suspicious.

I stole four salesbooks and took them home. I would bring some of the checks with me—I have two now—and when I would make a cash-take sale, I would write one of them using a charge account name I knew would be approved. I would have the merchandise wrapped and the check approved over the credit authorization board. When I got approval, I would tell the wrapper, but would not give her the check to enclose in the package. I would pocket the check and the money.

I would use some of these stolen checks to write out my own pass-outs to put on stolen merchandise, using a fictitious name. Other people told me how to eat for half price in the Cafe-

teria. I would take a sandwich, milk, and dessert and put it on one side of the tray, and a salad, roll, and coffee on the other side. I would tell the checker it was for two and then only pay one of the checks. Sometimes she would only issue one check and mark it with a red 2; then I couldn't get away with it.

I imagined myself as having an executive position and I resented the fact that my boss probably was earning three times as much as I was.

Well-educated people will attempt to beat any system and may succeed for a time. No matter how intelligent one is, some slip is made eventually.

Any procedure which will assure the issuing of a sales receipt to every customer, on each sale, will prevent delinquency and shrinkage.

One store in Buffalo, New York, has a program by which a cash award is presented to employes in recognition of good shopping reports. Employes are cautioned to enclose a receipt in all packages and a "no receipt given" report will eliminate a possible prize winner who has earned a creditable rating otherwise.

Chapter 15
RELEASE OR PROSECUTION

AN ARTICLE by Jon R. Waltz in the *Yale Law Journal*,[1] gave the official disposition of shoplifting cases in sixty-five cities during 1951. The report indicated that many persons apprehended while shoplifting were not prosecuted.

In 1944, and again in 1945, the detectives of one Chicago department store arrested two-thirds as many adult women for shoplifting as were formally charged with petty larceny of all forms (including shoplifting) by the police in the entire city of Chicago.

Store police cannot formally charge all persons arrested. Since testimony in court takes up the time of store detectives, department store staffs generally wish to prosecute as few arrested persons as possible. The problem is much the same for stores everywhere; therefore, there must be deliberate and concise screening of the persons to be jailed and prosecuted.

The English detective, Cecil Bishop, wrote in 1931 that:

> Arrests are made but few thieves are charged, for when a summons is issued the head of the department involved and at least one of his assistants, must attend the court, which means the staff is shorthanded for several days. An average of twenty thieves are caught weekly in a large department store, and were they all charged the directors would be faced with a total of at least 1,040 court cases a year. Suppose it were decided to proceed in all these cases and suppose an average of two witnesses were needed on each charge, and suppose in each case only two days were needed in arrangements and in attending court, the firm would still lose 4,160 working days in the year. It is obvious that under these circumstances no firm can afford to push a campaign against the shoplifter.[2]

---

[1] Waltz, Jon R.: Shoplifting And The Law Of Arrest: The Merchant's Dilemma, Reprinted from the *Yale Law Journal*, Volume 62, No. 5, April 1953.

[2] Bishop, Cecil: *Women and Crime*, Chatto and Windus, London, 1931, p. 6-7.

Release or Prosecution

In the Chicago Municipal Court, procedures are less time consuming, as a routine case usually requires about a half a day, but if continuances of the case are obtained, several man-days of detectives' time may be required.

All department stores face the problem of who is to be prosecuted and who not. Screening of shoplifters for release or prosecution must be done without bias.

If there is evidence of professionalism or commercialism, that is, if the arrested shoplifter is likely to be stealing merchandise in order to sell it, he should be charged formally.

The interrogator will look for inadequate identification, memorandums of merchandise to be stolen, pawn tickets, locker keys, etc. He will check for records of past arrests. He will consider behavior during pursuit and arrest proceedings, and any special equipment for stealing or concealing merchandise that the person may have with him. Close observation should be made for any evidence of narcotics addiction.

Professional shoplifters, narcotics addicts, and persons, who use force to resist apprehension, should be locked up and prosecuted. Arrest is sometimes used as a means of getting a severely disturbed neurotic or psychotic person to a source of adequate medical care as the court can, and sometimes does, refer persons to the psychiatric division.

If an apprehended person has no known previous record of arrest, is agreeable and cooperative, and if he can show adequate identification of his address, occupation, and will sign a waiver protecting the store against suit on false arrest charges, he can be released without prosecution.

The value of the merchandise stolen may also be a factor in determining the disposition of a case. Fifty per cent of shoplifters at all age levels take items of relatively small value. Twenty-five per cent of men however, take merchandise valued at $35 or more, and twenty-five per cent of all women are involved in the theft of merchandise of relatively large total value.[3]

Number and proportion of arrested shoplifters stealing merchandise at $20 or more, by age and sex:

[3] Cameron, Mary, Ph.D., Study.

Age[4]	Number of Males	Number at $20 or More	Per Cent of Age $20 or More
—15	100	2	2.
15–19	67	2	5.9
20–29	40	16	40.
30–39	29	9	31.
40–49	20	6	30.
50–59	26	9	33.
60–69	12	5	41.
70—	1	0	0.
Female			
—15	49	2	4.
15–19	127	17	13.3
20–29	140	29	20.
30–39	123	28	23.
40–49	163	46	38.
50–59	144	24	17.
60–69	45	4	9.
70—	30	0	0.

While a professional shoplifter may be arrested with merchandise under $20 in value, the majority of them will have much more. For most shoplifters the individual crime involves goods of such small value that it is very unlikely that the sale of the goods through illegal channels is the major consideration in committing the theft. The chart shows that a large portion of the people apprehended would be considered for release.

In a study of 709 adult women,[5] only 20 had records as having previously been arrested, and it was established that at least 7 of the 20 shoplifted commercially. This gives approximately 2 per cent of non-commercial women shoplifters that were arrested more than once. Among the men, 12 per cent had prior records. At least half of them were narcotic addicts or criminals by occupation, leaving about 6 per cent as a maximum proportion of non-commercial male shoplifters with more than one arrest.

Most shoplifters are "respectable" people. They are pilferers who may impulsively take an item of merchandise from stores.

The attitude of pilferers toward arrest is evidence of lack of

[4] *Ibid.*
[5] *Ibid.*

contact with criminal culture. Often pilferers do not think of themselves as thieves, yet frequently they will confess past thefts, detailing the time and the objects stolen.

If a pilferer is to be released, the interrogation procedure should be specifically and concisely aimed at breaking down any illusions he may have, that his behavior is regarded as merely "prankish." The promise should be made, and it should be kept, that if he is apprehended a second time, he will be locked up in jail and prosecuted.

Women especially, when released, should be advised to tell a parent, husband, or a doctor, if no other member of the family is a confidant. The reason is that women are more likely to fret over the incident.

One woman wrote the following after talking to her husband:

We are planning on coming into Chicago again on Tuesday. Would it be asking too much, to let me know what time would be most convenient for you to talk to us. It will have to be sometime after noon. May I thank you again for your very kindly attitude toward me. I will try and be more composed and not take up quite so much of your time.
Sincerely
Signed _____

Twenty years have elapsed without further contact.

Another letter from a shoplifter who was released:

I would like to tell you what happened to me after I left your store yesterday.

As I neared home I left the train and went into a company applying for a position. In almost a half hour I was employed. Then my conscience bothered me and I said that earlier in the day I had taken something in a store and been sent away for another chance. Instead of firing me I was given a split hour work so I can care for my darling children and a little extra income from someone who decided I was worth it.

With my cup overflowing I had this good news when the children came from school. Then last nite my husband called to say funds would come to me Saturday. I asked if he would just send himself instead and he said he would.

I write you this for many reasons. Just because it is from me and not the broken shell you saw—the real me. Secondly I know a broken home is desolate and without your help I could not have this family chance.

Thank you seems too little for what you have done for me. But I want you to know that whatever it was prompted your trust in me has not and never will be wasted.

I saw something so decent in your faces that it broke the lie I have been living for 2 months. I could not bear for anyone to find out my husband had gone so I said he was away on business. Telling you broke through to me.

One more thing. Your lady who stopped me said "I am a police officer" and smiled, even knowing *what I had done. I can't believe she is anything but an angel of mercy for being there to guide my footsteps when I needed it. She may have saved me from complete disaster and somehow I wish she knew how grateful I am to her.*

For your decency and trust I must say once more Thank you. *You will not ever be proven wrong.*

Sincerely yours,
Signed _____

The method of making an arrest, as described by this woman, is the best way to prevent excitement and even disorder. A gentle approach will usually disarm any shoplifter, amateur or professional, while a rough seizure or loud accusation may immediately put him on the defensive. At other times it may result in a nervous or hysterical condition accompanied by an involuntary discharge which may be embarrassing to both the arrestor and the arrested.

The following letter was from a woman who insisted on purchasing the merchandise she had stolen. Ordinarily I do not advise selling stolen merchandise unless it has been soiled or damaged in lifting. Then it may be a punishment to insist on payment. This woman had spent most of her day in town selecting the exact merchandise she wanted. I refused to sell her the merchandise while she was in custody, but sent her home to think it over, and told her that if she then decided she still wanted it, she might make a mail order purchase of it. She did not change her mind.

Enclosed please find a check for $152.84. I am also enclosing an itemized slip of items the check covers.

I owe you more than I really can express myself. Why isn't there more people like you. By being so nice—kind—and all things the lecture by itself was one no human being in right state of mind could and would not take it to heart and do the right thing.

I will never forget it as long as I live. It was a nightmare to me and I am wide awake to the fact. Thanks again and again for your kindness and you can rest assured that precious experience I will not waste.

Signed _____

Another case, one of many recommended to consult a doctor:

Following my experience with you yesterday, I called on my doctor, Dr. _____, and while he was not as definite as I would wish he did express confidence in helping me adjust my nervous condition, which he attributed to a physical ordeal I am undergoing, and encouraged me in the hope of restoring normal memory and conduct. I have placed myself under his treatment.

From my experience with you, may I add that I feel certain your management of the case will have a helpful effect in every way, and assure you of my deep gratitude.

Sincerely yours,
Signed _____

Nineteen years and no repeat of pilfering by the above, who lived in Chicago, at least no arrest.

I have received many letters and personal visits from persons who had been apprehended pilfering. There is never a repeat arrest of an individual who seemed to realize his problem.

It is rarely necessary to call the juvenile officers of the police department in on a case. Unless the juvenile is really bad, violent, or refuses to cooperate, a written report to the Juvenile Bureau will give the officers an opportunity to contact the parents and have the child brought to them if it is deemed advisable.

I advise that the parents or some member of the family be called while the juvenile is being detained and let the child take the phone and tell what he had done. It may be necessary to call a parent at work and ask him to call back on a public phone.

The composure of juveniles being detained has never ceased to amaze me, that is, until notified that they must tell a parent of to the public and that he never did find out what had happened to his own packages.

His wife testified that her husband was painting the kitchen when she left home, early that Saturday morning, with the baby, that she had instructed her husband to go to town later and buy a "toidy" seat for the baby and mail a package to his son who was in an army camp. She stated that when she returned home, he was not there, but a bottle of whisky which was partly filled when she left, was then empty.

The jury returned a not guilty verdict and shortly he filed a "false arrest" suit.

The store was the defendant in the civil suit which did not go to the jury. The plaintiff perjured himself by testifying that he had worked for a firm during a period when he was confined in the county jail. When the defense lawyer proved the perjury, the judge directed a verdict in favor of the store and dismissed the jury.

Since larceny is not just the taking and carrying away of someone's property but is the taking "with intent to steal," the State proved larceny by the fact that two packages were removed from a container in an area of the store posted "Employes Only." The conduct of the accused also indicated "intent to steal."

A person who is so intoxicated that he does not know what he is doing cannot be guilty of a crime requiring a "specific" intent. In this case the fact that the accused ran to escape indicated his realization that he was being followed, and even though the defense testimony in the criminal trial was intended to indicate drunkenness, there was no evidence of liquor indulgence noticed during interrogation.

The merchandise which was reported lost originally and which led to the arrest of the thief, was recovered from a public pay locker in a railroad station. The locker key was not found, but neither was his coat or jacket, which had probably been parked outside of the store.

Professional thieves or career criminals should be prosecuted whenever possible, even though the action inconveniences the store.

Chapter 16
STORE DETECTIVES ARE HUMAN

MAY I emphasize that I have associated with and employed many highly skilled and strictly honest and incorruptible store detectives; in fact, the majority can be so classed. Yet a small number, because of lack or weakness of inhibitions, yield to temptation.

Early in my protection service career it was pointed out to me that at least three ex-store detectives, from our city, were members of professional shoplifting groups. I have had the opportunity of interviewing all three of them subsequently, after arrest. I did not learn if they started their criminal career because of associates encountered during their employment, or if they obtained jobs in security work in order to help their associates' profession.

> The association which is of primary importance in criminal behavior is associated with persons who engage in systematic criminal behavior, a person who has never heard of professional shoplifting may meet a professional shoplifter, may become acquainted with and like him, learn from him the techniques, values, and codes of shoplifting, and under this tutelage may become a professional shoplifter, depending on his receptivity to the patterns of criminal behavior when presented to him.[1]

One woman was first arrested while working as a store detective in one of the smaller stores. A store detective from another store was arrested with her at that time. She has been arrested other times but my one experience with her was in 1944 when she was arrested with two other professional shoplifters. Three of our detectives and two city detectives made the arrest.

Merchandise on the persons of the three and merchandise recovered from lockers and check rooms, where they had de-

---

[1] Sutherland, Edwin H.: *Principles of Criminology*, 3rd edition, J. B. Lippincott Co., Chicago, Philadelphia, New York, p. 5.

posited it, totaled $922.64. It consisted of slips, housedresses, blouses, dresses, coats, infants wear, skirts, jackets, sweaters, hats, and suits; one day's work.

The ex-detective has not been arrested recently and I have been told that she has bragged that she now has a fool-proof system, that she can't be touched, that she hires her attorney by the year, that she works with store employes, through lockers and checkrooms, and that if her contacts do just as they are told, they probably won't be locked up even if they are caught. She has never had to use the attorney for her store contacts.

It is reported that she tells her customers to make a selection, take the style number, then call the order to her. One time we know of an overcoat that was selected, the order phoned to her home at night and by noon the next day she reported that it was the only coat of that style and that she could not get it because it would be missed.

One remark attributed to her was that she would not work with shoplifters because many of them are drug addicts and she doesn't want "undesirables" coming to her home and addicts will squeal when they are caught.

The *Saturday Evening Post* in its issue of April 23, 1949 ran an article, "Why Cops Turn Crooked,"[2] which reported realistically the story of the modern cop—the almost insurmountable pressure that is brought to bear on him from the underworld and the upperworld, sometimes operating in league with each other. The wonder is not that there are some crooked cops, but that there are so many honest ones.

The sincere and honest police officer, attorney, and judge, of whom there are certainly many all over the country in cities large and small, merit every respect and compliment in these times. It is significant that in communities where public officials are not corrupted or corruptible, crime does not prosper; in this way the criminal himself pays respect to the integrity of a public servant. In this discussion of crime from the criminal's standpoint, the corrupt official alone is under attack.

I have met many persons who wanted to buy their freedom,

---

[2] Wittles, David G.: Why Cops Turn Crooked, *Saturday Evening Post*, April 23, 1949.

after arrest. Often they are shoplifters, but at times they have committed other crimes.

One business executive, married and the father of grown children, who was apprehended exposing himself to women customers, offered any price for release.

Often criminals have offered detectives money in lieu of being taken to the protection office. One woman placed a $100 bill in the pocket of a detective while he escorted her to the protection office. When that did not cause him to release her arm and drop the traveling bag she had stolen, which he carried in his other hand, she offered $1,000 for her release.

An article which appeared in the newspaper a few days later explains why she offered $1,000 for her freedom.

> Orders Woman Back to New York. In Fur Gang Plot. Judge Grants Request for Extradition.
>
> .... attractive redhead and alleged associate of the phantom fur burglars, extradited to Garden City, Nassau County, New York, to face a charge of subornation of perjury.
>
> The hearing disclosed a strange plot in New York in which two alleged members of the fur theft gang were accused of paying $5,000 to an innocent man so he would confess that he, and not the actual thieves, was involved in a crime.

The article further stated that the woman and her husband "are suspected members of the fur burglary ring which has operated in New York, Chicago, Los Angeles, Miami, and major cities in Canada."

One well known shoplifter offered a detective $500 for her release. When the offer was turned down she stated that she had paid $500 each, to two men, for her release from a previous arrest.

During questioning at the detective bureau, with a State's Attorney's representative present, she explained what had occurred:

> Q. What happened outside there?
> A. We talked, and you know, taking the merchandise.
> Q. No I don't know, that is why I am asking you.
> A. We had a talk, and he still said nothing. I offered him $250.
> Q. For what?
> A. To make restitution for the stuff.

Q. What did he say to you?
A. He said you can't do it.
Q. All right, then what else was said?
A. After he said he couldn't do it, I had to go to jail. I gave the stuff up and said I will have to go to jail. He already had the stuff.
Q. Did you go inside the building then?
A. Yes.
Q. Did any further conversation take place outside before you entered the building?
A. No.
Q. Then what happened when you got inside the building?
A. I kept talking money.
Q. What do you mean by that?
A. I kept raising the price.
Q. You kept raising the price, what did you say?
A. Yes, I kept raising the price. I asked him what about $500 because there were two of them.

While my regular employes were not involved in this episode, the shoplifter was one who had been arrested in our stores, and might be again; and because of the temptation frequently presented to our personnel, all were requested to sign an agreement as part of their employment requirements.

> It is obvious that the honesty of an operator must be above question.
> Decisions that must be made in connection with the daily routine of business must be impartial and just, and the individual must be guided by the simple law of right, at all times. All investigations and reports must be absolutely truthful. Actions must be accompanied by the minimum of harshness or violence. Courtesy is expected.
> We are proud of the reputation our department has gained, not only with the law-enforcement agencies, courts, legal profession and our company associates, but also with the professional criminals that we expect to out-wit.
> Any wilful collusion or connivance of operators with criminals, accepting of bribes or illegal fees, or any other sharp or unethical practices will be cause for dismissal and possible criminal prosecution.

Store Detectives Are Human

Criminals will sometimes attempt to buy freedom with a tempting offer. Thieves who have nothing to lose can also make untruthful statements about an arrest, and have been known to dishonestly and maliciously accuse the arresting officer in hope of personal gain.

The company has confidence in its employes, but in order to maintain the high standards set by the department, and to protect the individual members of the department, any employe may be asked to voluntarily agree to a polygraph test, by a private operator, in the event circumstances make such a test desirable.

There has been no reason to follow up on these agreements since they were put into effect. Previously there were several unpleasant incidents.

At one time two promising young detectives reported following a "short-change manipulator." If they had seen everything they reported, I failed to understand why they did not place him under arrest, even though the crimes they reported seeing, occurred in neighboring shops. On investigation, I learned that they had stopped the man, and then during interrogation, they admitted that he had paid them off. They were both released.

A short-change manipulator will make a purchase for a small amount, probably $1, which he pays for with a $20 bill. His change is a $10 bill, a $5 bill and four $1 bills. Being a good conman, he continues his conversation with the salesperson while he slips the $10 bill into his pocket and produces a $1 bill which he places with the four single dollars, he had received, and then asks the salesperson to give him a five for the five singles.

While continuing his rapid fire conversation he will ask the salesperson for a $10 bill in exchange for the two fives. He receives the $10 bill but does not return the two fives, instead he hands the $10 bill originally received as change along with the last $10 bill and asks for a twenty.

By now the salesperson is usually confused to the extent that she does as requested and suffers $10 shortage.

The manipulator may start with a $10 bill and steal $5, or he may start with $50. Some of the salespeoples' cash shortages can be accounted for by this kind of a transaction, but unless the salesperson is aware of this kind of a confidence game, he will never associate the incident with his shortage.

One of the two incidents observed by the detectives, and for which the short-change artist paid off, was a transaction in silver money in a shoe shine parlor. He came out fifty cents to the good on that transaction.

I had two extremely distressing incidents. In both cases the detective was sent to the penitentiary—the first one for a hold up in the store, and the second one for a hold up outside.

An incident which occurred in the store on February 19, 1940 replaced the war news in the newspaper headlines.

Shortly after 12:30 p.m. the guard who escorted a money truck from one location in the store to another came to the office to report a holdup in an elevator.

Hunches and first impressions always justify further investigation in criminal inquiries. In this case I immediately felt that the guard was involved, and before he had fully explained what had happened, I ordered him to sit down while I made my investigation.

On further inquiry I learned that his account of the holdup tallied with that of the elevator and the cash division employe. The Chicago Police Department cooperated in the investigation to the point of assigning a plain clothes policeman to tail the guard.

What did happen can best be narrated as told in "Vanishing Gold, Will-O'-The-Wisp Clue of The Little Black Bag."[3]

> The holdup man confesses, after he and $15,721 of the $16,000 stolen had been captured and recovered, that he and the guard had both been cab drivers in another city in 1934.
>
> They had met in Chicago several months prior to the holdup, had a few drinks together, and made a date to meet again. At that time plans were laid for the holdup.
>
> The guard explained that he discovered that the lock on the strong box did not work at times. "We were supposed to pull the job three weeks ago. I went into the store, he saw me and put his hand behind his back for a second. That was a signal that the lock had worked that day and the job was off."

[3] Jay, John; Will-O'-The-Wisp Clue of The Little Black Bag, *Master Detective*. Sept. 1940.

"Last Monday I left the W.P.A. project sharp at noon on my lunch hour and took a street car to the store. I saw the guard push the hand truck. He pulled his hat a little lower on his head. That was the signal that everything was okay. I didn't have a gun. I just stuck my finger against his back."

"All I had to do was give the box a little jerk to open it. I put the bag under my vest and walked out of the store."[3]

The guard's past record was clear and he had a good record with the store for four years prior to temptation placed in his way when he accidentally discovered a defective lock.

An attractive young woman applied for a position as store detective. She had held a similar position in a New York store while her husband, a service man, was stationed in the east. Her references were satisfactory. Before her training period in our organization was completed, I received a telephone call one night, from the police who had placed her under arrest. The next day the newspapers carried headlines:

"DR. JEKYLL AND MRS. HYDE. NAB GIRL SLEUTH AS CAR BANDIT."
"ARREST WOMAN DETECTIVE IN HOLDUP CASE."
"MOTHER OF 5 KIDNAPPED IN CAR AND ROBBED."
"LIKES EXCITEMENT—GIRL SLEUTH ROBS."
"WAS LONELY AND BORED. GUN WOMAN ADMITS KIDNAPPING, HOLDUP. She said she was lonesome evenings with her husband away at camp, and turned to robbery as a diversion for the boredom of life in a one-room flat."

Crime, criminals, and law enforcement problems or the solving of crime is a fascinating subject to many people. This is proven by the interest of the public in newspapers, periodicals, books, plays, radio and television stories on the subject.

It is like a contest or a game, in that a detective is challenged continually, to outwit those who are trying to beat him.

Because people looking for the excitement of detective work are human, the same as all other employes, it is necessary to establish honesty standards in the Protection Department, and to enforce them.

Chapter 17
COOPERATION WITH OTHER AGENCIES

IN THE State of Illinois a store protection agent will exercise the arrest rights granted to private citizens and make an arrest for a criminal offense committed in his presence and which he himself witnessed. If the culprit is to be prosecuted he will be turned over to police officers with an arrest complaint signed by the store agent. The procedure is not that simple when an arrest is made by a police officer and store merchandise is recovered.

A news item reported that "store agents cooperate with police." Two men were arrested by police for the theft of sport coats from a store. At the time of arrest each one was wearing a stolen coat and, upon searching the felons, the police found in their possession a key to a public locker. The locker contained a portable radio and a traveler's clock which the arrested men admitted stealing from our store. The neighboring shop readily signed a complaint on the stolen coats. They had requested the assistance of the police, but we were unable to sign a complaint without first making a thorough investigation.

We first had to prove that the merchandise belonged to our store; we had to determine when it was last seen on display and when it was missed. Then records were checked to determine that no sale had been made between the time it was last seen and missed. If we could find witnesses we would then sign a complaint, even though the theft had not been witnessed by an employe. In this case the two men were found guilty and sentenced on each of the two counts of larceny, one for the stolen coats, the other for theft of the radio, which we could prove, their sentences to run concurrently.

A story in the *Police Digest,* April 1952, tells of how two officers on foot while their squad car was laid up for an overhaul, recovered a $95 suitcase for us. The officers spotted a shabbily clad man carrying a suitcase that appeared to be brand new and expensive. One of the officers remarked, "Nice bag you've got there." The man agreed and offered to sell it for a "Fin." The officer bargained and the selling price came down. Then, when the officers identified themselves, the man offered to give them the bag "if they'd just forget they'd ever seen him." A message requesting identity of the owner of the bag was sent out through the Retail Association. It was a brand and style carried in our luggage stock and investigation revealed it was missing from the selling floor. A complaint was signed.

A news item in a suburban paper told of our special officer being assaulted by two women who then escaped in a gray and black car driven by a black man. Police identified the Michigan license as being from Detroit.

Our detective had seen the two women shoplift women's wearing apparel which they concealed under their clothing. She followed the two from the store, expecting to meet a city officer to assist in taking them into custody. However, when they hesitated at the next corner the detective approached them. They dropped the wearing apparel, value $225, assaulted the detective and ran.

The license number of the car and description of the women were sent to the Detroit police, who returned photographs of suspects, known shoplifters, to the local police. After identifying two of the photographs the detective obtained arrest warrants. The Detroit police were notified of the warrants and after they had taken the shoplifters into custody our detective secured an extradition warrant from the State's Attorney's office to bring the fugitives back. She accompanied a policeman to Detroit and appeared before a judge there who honored the warrants. The stolen merchandise, which they had dropped, had been kept intact, to use as evidence in the local trial.

Stores can cooperate with other law enforcement agencies. An attempt was made to obtain a refund on an expensive sports shirt that had our label in it. The buyer knew that the shipment of shirts had never arrived in the store, so he delayed issuing a refund authorization until an "adjuster" arrived. The adjuster was a detective who secured enough information from the customer so that she could be located; then he told her we would hold the shirt until the sale could be verified. Because an interstate shipment had been stolen from a trucking company, the F.B.I. took over the investigation and was able to arrest the thieves.

Receiving platforms need close scrutiny. There have been truck drivers who, failing to unload a complete shipment, have stolen part of it. Drivers also have loaded other merchandise on their trucks while making a delivery. Once, when police made an arrest of a truck driver, they discovered a shipment of hoisery which had been consigned to our store. Our receiving records proved that the shipment had been in our possession and verified the confession of the driver that he had placed it in his truck while making a delivery to our receiving dock.

Another F.B.I. case was developed when we apprehended a part time employe stealing. Because of our investigation of other losses from the area where he worked, he was asked for permission to search his home. He gave a written authorization for us to remove anything we wished to investigate the ownership of.

The part time employe also had a full time job where he handled interstate shipments of merchandise. He admitted that some of the merchandise found in his home was stolen from his other place of employment. He confessed that he gave packages to one of the truck drivers who would keep some and drop some off at his home. A Federal case was made of it because some of the merchandise recovered was proven to have been lost in shipment.

Cooperation of store protection officers with other agents, besides stores, is sometimes helpful. For six days overcoats had been stolen from patrons of a restaurant in a local railroad station. On the seventh day the coat of a railroad special agent was stolen. The thief was apprehended as he was placing the coat in a public locker, where he had already concealed a purse and a pair of gloves, shoplifted from our store.

The 77 year old thief had a record of frequent arrests, dating from 1912, when he was first arrested for "horse theft."

Shoplifters sometimes pawn their loot, and also sometimes sell it to small antique or art ware shops. At times specific articles that have been stolen are reported to the police who check the pawn shops. Art objects or antiques are usually recovered because of the confession of a shoplifter who has been arrested. When art objects are lost it is a good bet to watch the art ware sections closely. One young man who was caught admitted previous thefts of art objects which were recovered with the assistance of the police. A painting, value $100, had been sold to an Art Gallery for $10. Antique silver had been sold to a silver shop. A jade necklace, $75, and a quartz snuff box, $150, were sold to a gift shop for $30, and a portable radio was pawned for $10.

In another case a number of articles, including antique Wedgewood pieces, were recovered from gift and antique shops. The pieces had been stolen by an employe who was apprehended because of two casual conversations. A gift shop owner happened to tell a store employe that a young man had brought a Wedgewood plaque to her, wanting to sell it for his aunt, but at a ridiculously low price. The employe just happened to tell one of the detectives of the conversation. The detective knew of losses of Wedgewood plaques, so she visited the shop owner. At the time, the woman could not find the young man's telephone number but gave a description of him, a description which could cover many individuals. Fortunately the shopkeeper later found the telephone number at her home and called our detective the next day. The young man was an employe, admitted his thefts, and a quantity of art objects were recovered from the shopkeepers who had purchased them from him.

The police cooperate on a robbery. "STORE ROBBERY IN LOOP. FIVE SHIRTS RECOVERED." A news item told of five squads from the Detective Bureau and the First District that went into action on a telephone report: "Holdup of department store at ———."

After entering the store with guns ready the police found themselves received only with surprise. They learned that a black boy had pilfered five shirts which he stuffed under his coat. He then dropped them, and while attempting a get away, a store officer stopped him. The commotion of his running, no doubt, prompted someone to report a holdup to the police.

The following chart, from the "Cameron Study," shows shoplifters with merchandise from other stores at the time of their arrest:

Shoplifters	Number with	Per Cent	Total Survey Cases
Men	3	2.4	147
Boys	10	6.3	159
Women	79	11.1	709
Girls	20	14.5	138
Total	112	9.7	1153

This is a recommendation for cooperation between stores: either through an association of Protection Agents; or an exchange of information between community stores.

Chapter 18
PROTECTION TASKS ARE KALEIDOSCOPIC

ALL THE tasks confronting a protection department of a larger store do not revolve around thefts; many are associated with colorful events, often dramatic in nature, while others are incidents that are pathetic or sorrowful. There are days when these events seem to flow in a continually changing form as though from a rotating tube.

Episodes that occur most frequently, and often are of momentous importance to the persons involved, are lost children, parents, or companions. Transportation schedules or important appointments are sometimes involved. Adults or elderly lost persons are sometimes more difficult to locate than children because they are reluctant to ask for help.

Lost mothers can be a greater problem than lost children due to a desire to search. Few of the hundreds of lost children, in a year, are lost for long. If the adult will stay in one place it is easy to send the child to her or her to the child.

An experience of years ago has made it easy for me to assure frenzied parents that their missing offspring will be found.

When a six year old boy had been missing for more than six hours and he had not been found by store closing time, I was probably as apprehensive as the parents. The boy became separated from his mother, on the toy floor, before noon. When he had not been found within a reasonable period of time, the father was called and being a sensible man, he sent the mother home in case word of the boy's whereabouts arrived there.

Everything possible had been done during the afternoon and the police had been contacted to join in the search. Arrangements were made to hold a number of employes after store hours to search every nook and cranny that could hide a small boy. Shortly after seven o'clock we received the joyful news, from the mother, that the boy had arrived home.

Underwriters will help in determining the adequacy of the watch service. A central station watchmen's service will more than likely have training material available for watchmen, and there are books dealing exclusively with plant protection. *Industrial Plant Protection*[5] covers guard duties thoroughly and should be studied by anyone having the responsibility for hiring and training guards.

Watchmen and guard duties are sometimes combined, that is the night time employe not only watches over the store after it is closed, but he may also have the responsibility for dealing with people. He may inform the public that the store has closed and check employes and packages out of the store, or he may check employes in before the store opens. He may be assigned certain duties for enforcing store rules that will classify the job as a "guard" rather than a "watchman."

Protection tasks are kaleidoscopic, rare and extremely varied incidents occur wherever crowds gather. Emergency illnesses require attention. Doctors, the fire department, a pulmotor squad, or a priest may be required. Police are summoned in case of a sudden death. Store personnel should be capable of meeting any crisis.

The contribution that all phases of protection can add to a successful and profitable retail operation should be thoroughly considered by the management of every store.

[5] Davis, John Richelieu: *Industrial Plant Protection*, Charles C Thomas, Publisher, Springfield, Illinois, 1957.

Chapter 19

ROBBERY—BURGLARY

"Gun Terrorizes Cashier."
"Gunman Robs Driver, Two Aids; Steals Truck."
"Police Seize Two Who Confess 20 Robberies."

Headlines, such as these, appear in newspapers daily. Occasionally a story, detailing a robbery, will relate how a shopkeeper successfully routed robbers, but too often we read of the loss of life due to resistance.

> Bandits plotting a stick-up job have precisely the same deeply rooted feelings of kindness toward their victims, that a pair of brass knuckles would have. So let's be practical, Mr. Citizen.
>
> Yesterday, or the day before, it was some other fellow's misfortune to be slugged on the street, or to have his place of business burglarized, or his wife attacked in her home.
>
> Tomorrow, or the day following, your own number may come up to play the lead role in one of these crime dramas, for today's criminals play no favorites in selecting their victims for the morrow. It is enough that you have something they want.[1]

Advice—straight from convicts—that may save your life. Regardless of what the story books may infer, it is better to be a live dope than a dead hero.

Fifty-four robbers say: "Don't argue with a 'nervous' gun."[2]

Store personnel, who are responsible for handling large sums of cash or valuable merchandise, and shop cashiers should be instructed in actions to be followed, in case of a "holdup."

Stores, small and large, should invest in suitable protection for valuables, as well as personnel. Built-in safes are available. In

---

[1] *Law of the Jungle*, Public Safety Department, Acme Markets—American Stores, Philadelphia, Pennsylvania.

[2] Hartlep, Felix: Number 44068, Louisiana Penitentiary, How to Keep from Getting Murdered, *American Weekly*, Hearst Publishing Co., Inc., New York, 1955.

the larger cities an armored collection service is at hand and store employes do not know the combination to the safe.

A central alarm service may be had in many cities. Vaults, safes, windows, doors, fire escapes, and all hazardous areas can be wired so that any intrusion or tampering will send an alarm to a central office. Some alarm systems can be triggered by a cashier without noticeable effort.

In some smaller communities it is possible to have an alarm system connected by telephone wires to a local police station. Such an installation can result in the capture of burglars or robbers, as indicated in the newspaper account of a jeweler and an optometrist who were held up. "Burglars' Victims Push Silent Button And Four Are Seized." As the two victims, and a customer, were being herded into a rear room at gunpoint, one of them sounded the alarm. Police who answered the alarm foiled the robbery and arrested three men and a woman, bandits.

All stores should consider all possible means for protecting valuables from burglars and holdup men. Because burglars and robbers are often professionals, skilled in their trade, it seems to be an impossibility to entirely rule out the chance of any store being visited by these unpredictable guests. It is therefore also advisable for all merchants to consider holdup and burglary insurance.

These criminals may be classified as professionals due to repeated arrests for the same type of offense. Statistics have been published showing that 63 per cent of the persons arrested for robbery, in one year, had previously been arrested for the same offense. Many of the remaining percentage were, no doubt, youths who might wield a "nervous Gun."

Under any circumstances, employes should be instructed to follow the criminals' directions exactly, if held up by armed or apparently armed persons.

The victim of a holdup should be cooperative in putting up hands or lying face down and should control his acts carefully so as not to make any sudden noises or moves that might be misinterpreted. If alarms to summon help are installed they should be arranged so that they can be operated without noticeable movements.

Robbery—Burglary

Bandits sometimes develop distinctive habits of operation. As soon as a person realizes a holdup is occurring, and as long as he is allowed to face the robber, he should be making mental notes of the appearance or any peculiarities that may give the police clues.

Very few people can accurately describe individuals but it can be determined that one is short, average, or tall in height. He may be described as slender, fat, average, muscular, and any deformity should certainly be noted. The age may be estimated, color of hair noted, and variations in appearance of eyes, nose, mouth, ears, or teeth may help in a possible later identification.

Pay particular attention to speech. Note any accent, impediment, and try to remember the words of the command.

If a weapon is used, in addition to noting its appearance, a victim may have a better opportunity to observe the hands more closely than other features. They may be distinctive in appearance.

Any person under the stress and strain of a holdup may not be expected to see many of the identifying features of the criminal, but he should remember any one or a few of the characteristics noted. Any clue may help the police to locate the perpetrator or may help in making a positive identification in viewing police pictures or suspects.

Report a robbery to the police as soon as possible. Look for any witnesses who may have noticed the robber or robbers, their car, or method of escape. Then as soon as possible make written notes of all the information that can be remembered.

Any employe answering an alarm or observing a holdup or robbery can be of most assistance by notifying the police, observing the bandit and the get away car, without attracting attention. Rushing to the assistance of the victim may cause someone to get hurt.

One acquaintance of mine lost his life when he attempted to stop a holdup man. After the holdup of a shop, during busy hours of the day, the victim and pedestrians pursued the robber, shouting "stop that man." A fatal shot was the answer to the innocent man who attempted it.

Preparations previously made can also mean the death of

in the shop waiting. This was one of the rare occurrences when a robbery was prevented because of a tip off.

Some lock manufacturers are incorporating new safety measures into locks. One newer model has an extra long bolt that swings from a horizontal to a perpendicular position. This model can be installed in a relatively narrow door frame but the longer bolt prevents the door jam being pried away to release the bolt.

Time recording locks have many uses. At least one manufacturer can supply numbered keys and the record of entry will identify the key used to open the lock, as well as the date and time it was unlocked. They are useful for stores, warehouses, or other properties, for which keys are given to more than one individual. They can also serve a useful purpose on some stockrooms; for example, they might be used on a liquor stockroom in a restaurant or food operation.

It is not practical to describe here all the alarm systems in detail because modern electronics and science are developing and perfecting new ideas. It can be said that there are many types of protective alarms, including ultrasonic, that have been developed and can be installed so as to be an asset to a store protection service.

In years past, some investigators used a dry chemical that would leave an indelible stain on damp hands, in an attempt to trap pilferers. It was not always successful. One sure way of catching a thief was to arrange a "plant," or hiding place, and keep a man in it to watch an area suffering loss.

A few years ago, the manager of a section, selling small but valuable merchandise, reported a suspicion of losses. His merchandise was kept under lock and key and only displayed in quantities that were easily watched. A survey of the section personnel did not uncover any suspects. The manager was advised to arrange the stock in drawers in a pattern, before leaving at night, so that when he opened the drawers in the morning, he could determine if it had been disturbed. There were several indications of tampering over a two week period.

A "plant" was arranged on top of some fixtures and a man occupied it soon after the store closed. Working the job was a crafty process. The watcher kept under cover, then had to sneak his reliever in while he slipped out of a door, which was never used during the hours the store was closed.

The news of any unusual activity of the protection department personnel at night travels the "grapevine" rapidly, even in a large store. This investigation was successful.

On the second shift of the fourth night, a mopper pushed his truck into the room and left it stand in the middle aisle near the room entrance. He walked to the west side of the room, then to the south end, over to the east side, back north and over to the truck. He then pushed the truck to the other end of the room and again left it. After looking around, and apparently determining that the way was clear, he walked to a counter, reached over the case and tried the door. It was locked. So was the next door that he attempted to open.

His next move was to cross an aisle, then go behind a counter and try to open drawers that were all secure. His efforts did not stop there. Behind another counter he pulled on drawers and one of them opened. Two small pieces of merchandise were removed and secreted in his pocket.

All merchandise in this room might be a temptation to a weak individual. Much of it could be concealed easily in clothing. The locks were found to be worn and insecure. Was a major alteration advisable or could the room be protected with alarms?

An experiment with an ultrasonic alarm system proved that the movement of a person entering the room could alert a guard stationed in another part of the building. The installation of the equipment was less costly than replacement of all the locks and it also furnished additional protection.

The heat waves generated by a small piece of paper burning in a pan will set off the alarm. In case of a fire in the room, the guard could be on the scene in ample time to obtain aid before sprinkler heads fused and flooded the room. It would also alert the guard if a prowler entered the room.

The ultrasonic alarm can be sent to a local police station via telephone hook up. Such an arrangement enabled a suburban police force to catch an intruder in a local hardware store.

Photographs taken with infra-red flash bulbs have been used to trap night workers in stores. The camera can be concealed

168   *Shoplifting and Shrinkage Protection*

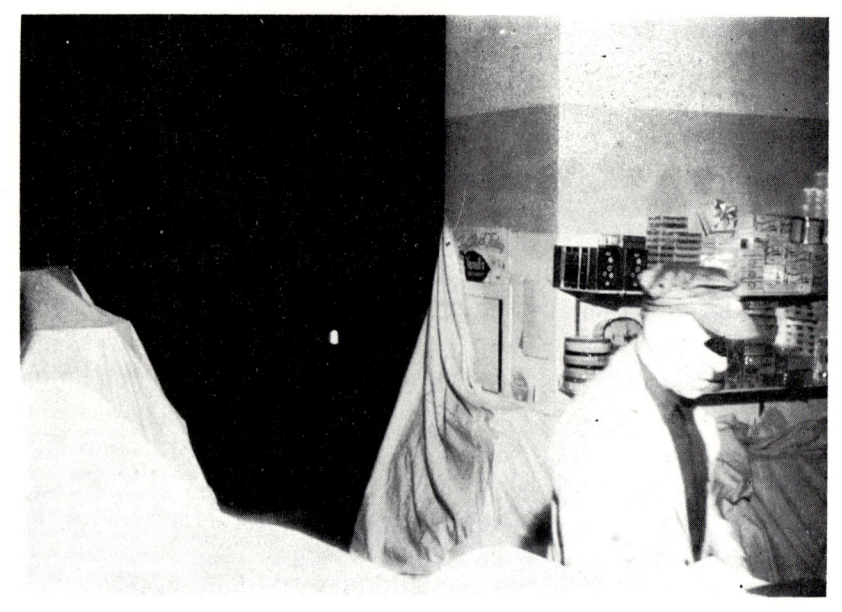

A night time worker photographed when he broke a fine wire and triggered an infra-red flash bulb. The black background is area that remained in darkness.

behind a glass shield and various gadgets can be arranged to snap the picture. The pilferer is unaware that his picture is being taken.

Closed circuit television cameras and monitors are useful for some security jobs. Good equipment is costly and it is somewhat difficult to scan a large area. "Plants" are more useful for locating shoplifters.

A "plant" can be improvised; that is a watcher may conceal himself temporarily behind existing equipment, or they can be perpared so that troublesome spots can be surveyed from time to time. Slits or peep holes can be made in fixtures, or stockroom or office walls; grill work can be used on balconies or in walls. Special booths, built around posts or planned as part of the section fixtures, with a two way mirror that allows one to see a lighted area from a dark one, are useful. A door for a quick exit should be provided.

Radar has been developed for night time protection. A unit weighing thirty-four pounds, using electric current equal to that

Locks—Alarms—Plants 169

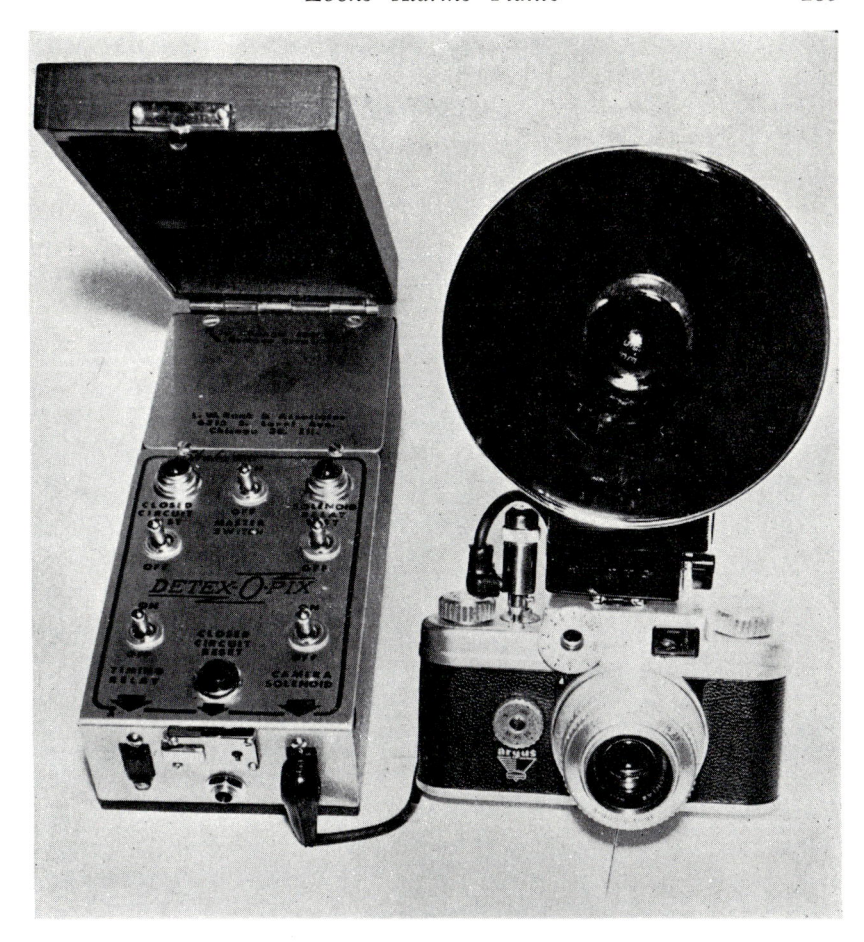

used by a 60 watt bulb, can be hooked up with various protective devices. The unit can be concealed yet completely saturate a room, so that an intruder cannot escape detection. This unit can operate local alarms, be connected to a central office by a special telephone connection, switch on floodlights, or operate a camera.

If an intruder has been frightened off, the radar unit automatically resets itself after a minute; otherwise the alarm will continue if he remains. If the set, the cable, or the electricity is tampered with, the alarm goes off automatically.

Burglar alarms of all kinds are useful. Burglars were apparently scared away from a loan company quarters when they set off an alarm. Police and watchmen, who answered the alarm from a central office, did not find the intruders but they did find holes had been cut in the ceiling from the second floor, and holes in the roof of the third floor, in an attempt to by pass alarms while gaining entrance to the premises.

Two stories on burglaries appeared in the Sunday paper as this is being written. They are typical of news items appearing daily throughout the nation and highlight the need of protection for merchants.

One story told of police halting an unlighted car, in which they found a safe, stolen an hour earlier from a suburban sporting goods store. The driver, who was locked up, is quoted as saying, "How in the world did that get into my car?"

The other item is an account of a nine man gang seized in a police trap. The gang had recently taken approximately $50,000 in loot in burglaries from three other companies. Entrance to the building was made by breaking the lock off the rear door. Two rented trucks had driven up to the loading dock to be used to haul away the stolen goods.

The need for fast protective communications is sometimes handled by two way radiophones. They may be used successfully on some investigations but are too cumbersome for store detectives to use.

An electronic communication system, far superior to the bell signals used in the past, can locate any one individual touring a store. A store detective, maintenance man, or an executive can carry a pocket size radio receiver and receive a message sent from a central location, either a switch board or from the protection office. It is not difficult to wire a building because the sound waves carry quite a distance.

Protection systems, of one kind or another, are available. In the interest of shrinkage prevention, merchants should review their loss possibilities, consider their insurance coverage, and the possible inconvenience to the business that a burglary might entail, then shop for the protection system most suited to the needs of the business.

Chapter 21
WATCHDOGS

Ask a glamorous celebrity where a woman can find true love and she may tell you that men are fickle, but once a dog gives his heart—it means forever and a day.

Dogs fill a great need in the lives of many ordinary folk—they certainly can fill a need in business life as watchdogs, or as reported in *Life*:[1] "Growling Guards," "watchdogs use bells and barks to protect store from burglars."

The use of watchdogs is not unique; they have been used for protection since time immemorial and they performed valuable service for our armed forces. Reading about war dogs caused me to think that they might solve some of my protection problems, especially when our post war economy made it increasingly difficult to keep our night guard force manned.

One of our warehouses consisted of two long buildings connected at one end, but separated by a railroad spur and receiving platform that ran between them. If the floor area had been contained in one building, instead of two, one watchman could have toured the building. As it was, two men were required for each shift.

I couldn't rebuild the building, but maybe one man could travel both buildings at the one end where there was a connecting passageway, and let dogs do some of the legwork down through the building. If a program of this kind was decided on it would have to be a professional one, not amateur.

I discussed the use of dogs with trainers, veterinarians, and a dog psychologist. I talked with everyone that I thought might help me. All the information that I gathered convinced me that dogs would be useful on our protection force, and while other breeds could be used, it was decided that German Shepherds would best serve our purpose.

[1] *Life*, March 10, 1952.

part of the building would stop at the window and bark. It was learned the following day that a watchman in a building across the street had seen a man, carrying what looked to be a pinch bar, run from the vicinity of the window picked out by the dogs.

At one time a guard, upon investigating a disturbance of a dog, discovered a ballast burning out in a flourescent lamp on a stairway.

A dog can also guard an area by being chained to a cable which gives him an opportunity to travel the entire length of a receiving dock or other area that may need special protection.

On Patrol

A holdup of a warehouse cashier and the loss of a Christmas, extra help, payroll resulted in two protective measures: the substitution of checks for cash for payroll in outlying areas, and a dog stationed with the guard at the truck dock door.

One thing about protection is that if the problems are licked at one place, something crops up at another.

There have been reports from various cities of night losses apparently due to some thief who has concealed himself in a store before closing time.

At one time a watchman reported a prowler in the store about 4 a.m. Police and protection personnel were called and a search of the premises was made but the prowler was not discovered.

Some nights later a watchman discovered a man packing two corrugated cartons with merchandise from racks on a selling floor. The culprit also saw the watchman and fled to a window and down a fire escape. He outdistanced the watchman and made his escape.

After that, German Shepherd dogs were secured and started training for guard work in the store, but before they were ready to be put to work, the thief, an ex-employe, was caught. He was sentenced to a year in jail; even so dogs were put to work patrolling the store during the night. They will search through all out of the way areas while working under the direction of a guard.

A dog will give an alarm if a guard is being followed by another person and by watching the actions of the dog the guard will know if a human is in an area that they are approaching. The dog will give an alert before he barks. The guard only needs to watch the dogs' stance, head, and ears for that alarm.

An informative article, "Dogs in War, Police Work and on Patrol," by Charles F. Sloane, appeared in *The Journal of Criminal Law, Criminology and Police Science,* Volume 46, Number 3, September-October, 1955 (Northwestern University School of Law).

Sleep, during the still of the night, can be more peaceful for the store or protection manager who knows that he has the additional protection of watchdogs.

Chapter 22

SHOPLIFTING LAWS—PENALTIES

PRIOR to a new shoplifting law effective July 1, 1957, Illinois merchants faced the danger of a law suit for false arrest if they detained an innocent person. In case of arrest or detention it was necessary to prove to a court or a jury that a crime actually had been committed in the presence of the arrester, and that the arrested person was guilty. Failure to do this, and if prosecution should fail, the merchant could be liable for false arrest or false imprisonment, and be required to pay civil damages. For this reason, some merchants, including nationally known retail organizations, took no action against shoplifters.

The laws of many of the states similarly restrict merchants in the protection of their property; however some states recognize a middle ground which can be used as a partial solution to the shoplifting problem, while at the same time preserving the rights of a person arrested.

This middle ground allows a merchant to detain a person if he has probable cause, not mere suspicion, for believing that the person detained has unlawfully appropriated merchandise. The detention must be accomplished in a reasonable manner and must be limited to a reasonable time.

Shoplifting had risen in Illinois until it was estimated that "each year shoplifters help themselves to more than $80 million worth of merchandise from the stores. . . ." In order to help combat the loss, to merchants, the retailers associations prepared material pointing out that theft on so gigantic a scale must eventually affect the consuming public to whom this loss must be translated in the form of higher retail prices. The presentation outlining the legislative problem stated:

> Inventory shrinkage in retail stores averages about 1.5 per cent of sales. Retail sales in Illinois, according to the 1954 census

of Business of the United States Bureau of the Census, amounted to $11,018,913,000 during the year. Assuming half of the merchant's inventory loss is attributable to theft then the loss to Illinois merchants from that cause was $82,641,847 in 1954.

"A Bill-For an Act in relation to shoplifting" was introduced in the Legislative General Assembly in 1957. It was passed and signed into law by the Governor effective July 1, 1957.

Section 3 of House Bill No. 333, 1957, Illinois, interprets the object and purpose of the statute:

> Any merchant, his agent or employee, who has probable cause to believe that a person has wrongfully taken or has actual possession of and is about to wrongfully take merchandise from a mercantile establishment, may detain such person in a reasonable manner and for a reasonable length of time for the purpose of investigating the ownership of such merchandise. Such reasonable detention shall not constitute an arrest nor shall it render the merchant, his agent or employee, liable to the person detained.

North Carolina merchants had attempted but were unsuccessful in having a similar law passed, giving them detention powers. It was estimated that shoplifters were responsible for loss costing the merchants of that state $30 million a year. They were favored with a new law, in 1957, which replaces the only previous protection, a petty larceny law.

The new law in North Carolina is patterned after the Maine law, which specifies the merchandise must be on the person.

The North Carolina law carries a $100 fine, six months imprisonment, or both, for goods found concealed "upon or about" a person. The "about" would take care of bags in which merchandise might be concealed.

Placards calling attention to the new law are made available to merchants through their association. Merchants are also running ads calling attention to the new law. The new law is hoped to at least be a psychological factor in reducing shoplifting in the state.

The Supreme Court of California was probably the first court to accept probable cause as a defense to a detention made for the purpose of investigating the ownership of property in a shoplifting case.[1]

> In an effort to harmonize the individual right to liberty with a reasonable protection to the person or property of the defendant, it should be said in such charge for false imprisonment, where a defendant had probable cause to believe that the plaintiff was about to injure defendant in his person or property . . . that probable cause is a defense, provided, of course, the detention was reasonable.

Supreme Court decisions in a few other jurisdictions indicate that, while probable cause is a question of fact, if the facts of the detention are reasonable, the probable cause will defend a detention by merchants for the investigation of the ownership of property.

No specific recommendations are made for Illinois merchants until the Supreme Court of the State has accepted the "probable cause;" however, it can no doubt be assumed that a mere request, not force, would not result in a court awarding damages for detention.

The Ohio Court held that the actions of a store manager did not amount to false arrest or false imprisonment when he approached a customer and said, "Madam, that bag will have to be searched." The court said:[2]

> It (meaning the defendant company) thought its private right of property was being violated, which it was resisting. It was not assuming to vindicate any public right. The plaintiff was not accused of any crime. Nothing was done to indicate that she was being held for delivery to a peace officer to answer a criminal charge. Under such circumstances there is no basis for the suggestion that this is a false imprisonment, indicated by false arrest.

The primary reason for citing these laws is to point out to the reader that there is a decided difference in the laws of various states. There is little variety in the methods of shoplifting, the delinquency pattern or the problems of storekeepers.

[1] Collyer v S. H. Kress Co. 54P (2) 20, 1936.
[2] Lester v Albers Super Markets. Ohio Appeals 114 N.E. (2) 529, 1952, p. 532.

Shoplifting, in Illinois, may be either a felony, "Grand Larceny," or a misdemeanor, "Petit Larceny." In this state $50 has been the dividing line between the two since July 1951. A misdemeanor complaint may be signed for a stolen article with a value in excess of $50 by indicating a value of $49.95, or less, in the complaint. This practice is sometimes advisable, especially where the retail value of merchandise does not greatly exceed $50.

The stealing of money from the person of another—picking a pocket—is a felony regardless of the amount stolen.

Under the Criminal Code of Illinois, a felony, or grand larceny, is punishable with a penitentiary sentence of 1-10 years. A misdemeanor, or petit larceny, is punishable with a sentence not to exceed 1 year in the county jail. In shoplifting convictions the judge is empowered to grant "probation" under certain conditions. The court may require that restitution, for the amount of a theft, be made during the probation period, as one of the conditions for the convicted person remaining at liberty.

Punishment for an individual can exceed the penalty imposed by the court. Upon her release from serving a ninety day sentence for shoplifting, one woman reported that her upper front teeth had been knocked out during a fight with another inmate. The quarrel was precipitated over the use of a wash tub.

Self imposed punishment often torments persons apprehended shoplifting but not prosecuted. The mental anguish, that sometimes comes with realization of the seriousness of the act, affects the well-being of some people as much as prosecution could have done.

No matter what state a business is conducted in; regardless of release or prosecution; protection policy should be established and conducted so that if there is an acquittal of the defendant in a criminal court; followed by a civil suit for damages; or if an error is made in detaining a person; the store can defend any action brought against it so as to keep any damages to the minimum. Anyone can file a civil suit for damages, and in every case of litigation, there must be a loser. The store does not want to be a large loser.

A local jeweler was, no doubt, within his rights when he questioned a "customer." He had seen her put a $1,200 diamond ring in her purse. His request for it evoked a denial that she had taken it. He did not use violence; in fact he did not lay a hand on her, but he did insist that she look in her purse, because he had seen her place it there. She returned the ring and left without further ado.

This investigation for possession of the ring seemed to have been conducted in a "reasonable manner and for a reasonable length of time," therefore, under the new Illinois act would "not constitute an arrest nor shall it render the merchant, his agent or employe, liable to the person detained."

An Illinois Statute states:[3]

> False imprisonment is an unlawful violation of the personal liberty of another, and consists in confinement or detention without sufficient legal authority.

In order to constitute false imprisonment it is not necessary to show the person guilty thereof used physical violence or laid hands on the person falsely imprisoned or confined him in a jail or prison, but it will be sufficient if at any place or time he in any manner restrained such a person of his liberty or detained him from doing what he desired.

When a wrong is committed by an agent or employe in the course of his employment, and while pursuing his employer's business, the employer will be liable for any damage resulting from such wrongful act, although it is done without the employer's knowledge or consent, unless the wrongful act is a wilful departure from such employment or business.

The plaintiff in a false arrest suit can be an employe or any person claiming illegal restraint of his liberty.

An employer has the right to question an employe during regular working hours. The interrogation might even be in regards to a theft. With reasonable cause, a request can be made of the employe to submit samples of hand writing or to take a lie detector test. There should be no physical restraint, and no threats of bodily harm or restraint.

If the interrogator acts in good faith and with honest intentions and with proper caution, then the restraint, if any, should not be

---

[3] Section 252 of Chapter 38, Smith-Hurd, Illinois Revised Statutes.

considered unlawful and there should be no false imprisonment in the case.

One of the few false arrest decisions in litigation of an employe vs. a store employer, is a Wisconsin decision:[4]

Plaintiff, an employe of the defendant sued her employer for false imprisonment, slander, and assault. A jury found for the defendant on the charge of assault and found for the plaintiff on the charge of false imprisonment and slander. The trial court set aside the verdict of the jury with respect to slander, but rendered judgment in favor of the plaintiff on the verdict for false imprisonment. On appeal, the Supreme Court of Wisconsin reversed the trial court and remanded the case with directions to dismiss the plaintiff's complaint.

The plaintiff had been called to the office of the assistant superintendent. He was in conference with another party and she was told to sit down and wait until he was free to see her. When the other party left, the official closed the door to his office. This door had a self-lock so that it could not be opened from the outside without a key, but could be easily opened from the inside. She was questioned regarding the taking of money for her own use, and the failure to make out sales slips.

In reaching its decision the Supreme Court said:

> . . . False imprisonment is defined to be "the unlawful restraint by one person of the physical liberty of another." "The true test seems to be, not the extent of the restraint, but the unlawfulness thereof."
>
> In the instant case, an employer summoned to his office an employee for an interview concerning matters coming to the attention of the employer casting doubt upon the fidelity of the employee. The office was small, but it was a regularly established office of the employer. The interview was somewhat prolonged, but during the entire period, the time of the employee belonged to the employer. She was compensated for every minute of the time spent by her in the office. Her time was under the employer's direction and control. . . .
>
> . . . It readily may be conceived that such interviews may be held at improper places, at improper times, and conducted in

[4] Weiler v Herzfeld-Phillipson Co., 189 Wis. 554, 208 N.W. 599.

an improper manner. We cannot conceive, however, that the place in which this interview was conducted can have any bearing whatever upon the question of unlawful restraint. . . .

. . . While employers should be admonished that their dealings with their employes under such circumstances must be reasonable and humane, we cannot adopt a rule putting an employer in jeopardy of a charge of false imprisonment when he summons to his office for an interview an employee whose conduct is unsatisfactory, or whose fidelity is under suspicion, especially where the office is one in which the employer customarily does his business, and the period of the interview is within the time for which the employee is being compensated by the employer. We conclude that the record discloses no evidence sustaining the findings of false imprisonment.

Other decisions in litigation between employe and employer, for unlawful violation of personal liberty are:[5]

A law may be a desirable psychological device for the prevention of loss, such as Bill 333, but it alone is not the solution to shrinkage. Every merchant should learn first the rights of citizens; then the principles of the law as it applies to his rights, in the protection of his property, in his jurisdiction; then determine his loss hazards and exercise all legal means for correction.

[5] Davis & Allcott Company v Rosa Booser, 215 Ala. 116, 10 Sp. 28.
Amborn v Smyser, 182 Ill. App. 208, at 209.

Chapter 23
INVESTIGATION

INVESTIGATION, a searching inquiry in order to ascertain facts, and the process of elimination, are the means by which shrinkages are resolved, perpetrators of crimes apprehended and convicted, and evidence is collected to defend civil lawsuits.

Criminal investigation is a detailed and careful examination of all hunches, tips, suspicions, clues, or evidence, in order to assemble facts to prove the definite existence of guilt. In order to find the guilty it is often necessary to check out or eliminate the innocent from any suspicion.

There have been numerous references to, and many of the cases mentioned herein were uncovered due to, investigations.

Shoplifters are arrested on the basis of observation and physical evidence. Interrogation is a prominent part of investigation, so everyone arrested is questioned. It is essential that certain background facts be learned about an individual before a decision can be made to release or prosecute.

The investigation should proceed with all possible promptitude, because an arrested person should not be detained any longer than necessary to determine the further action to be taken.

The investigator must know the law of evidence—it must be obtained by lawful means; it must be admissible evidence and presented properly in court. A confession secured under duress will not be admissible in court; neither will evidence secured by illegal search. In Illinois, a person arrested may be searched to permit recovery of the stolen goods in his possession, also for any concealed weapons. His clothing, body, handbag, packages, or the immediate surroundings, including an automobile, may be searched. If the arrest is legal, the property recovered in the search may be used as evidence; however, if the arrest should be illegal, the search could constitute a technical assault and battery.

Questioning of a suspected employe should be done during his regular working hours, and he should not be compelled to remain in confinement, unless he is to be formally arrested and charged with a crime. Employes will almost always voluntarily submit to interrogation if approached in the proper manner.

Interrogation of any person who has stolen is more than asking questions. A thief is likely to be inclined to also lie either from embarrassment or fear of the consequences. It is difficult to set any special rules for an investigator to follow in interrogation because no two individuals react in exactly the same way. Successful results will be due to the resourcefulness of the investigator.

It is not necessary to threaten, promise, or lay a hand on the accused. One who may expect rough treatment will usually respond to suaveness on the part of the questioner, especially if the interview is conducted on a level of mutual understanding and not with a superior attitude.

The investigation of a shoplifter can start at the point of arrest. Preparation for further speedy interrogation can start then. One approach used by a detective when she stopped a woman who had removed an empty paper bag from her purse and dropped a canned ham in it was: "Weren't you afraid that ham would break through the bag?" "Oh no, I knew it wouldn't." "We will go to the office but no one will know that you are under arrest; I will just take your arm. By the way—how old are you?" "65 ——— etc." The shoplifter was most cooperative, in answering questions, upon reaching the office. She was a housewife from a town about 90 miles away and she carried $550 on her person.

Persons in custody commonly try to exact a promise of the disposition of their case before giving any information. In order to be competent evidence a confession must be obtained voluntarily and not procured by pressure. A threat, especially if coupled with some indication of benefit to the accuser, may render a confession involuntary. The investigator must refuse any promise of leniency and decline to make an agreement in order to obtain a confession.

Tactfulness on the part of the examiner will often produce information that will be useful in further investigations of loss. Friendly conversations with professional shoplifters have even developed information of other shoplifters and their method of operation. A great deal can be learned from shoplifters that will help prevent shrinkage. One once said that she boosted in a certain section at the same time every day. She had discovered that there was no protection or supervision in the area at that time. Investigation proved her point; the habits of the section personnel left it unprotected at that time of the day.

The character and ability of every prospective employe should be investigated. The application should be complete enough to account for prior employment and former addresses. Any periods of unemployment should be questioned. An experienced personnel interviewer may discern some circumstances that would suggest a further investigation before hiring an applicant. Some jobs may warrant a special type of investigation.

Letter inquiries for reference might be satisfactory for some companies and some jobs. Any discrepancies in employment dates or other facts might justify personal contacts. It is recommended that all references be requested in writing rather than by telephone, and all written references presented by the applicant should be verified.

Credit references are sometimes desirable. Finger printing of employes serves a purpose and questioning for arrests helps to eliminate employment of some undesirable people. The merchants in some cities have a clearing house that handles the problems of common interest.

Some lie-detector operators conduct personnel investigations of applicants. Some laboratories furnish a form to the applicant, that includes many questions regarding his honesty, to be completed before the test is run.[1] After the laboratory examiner has evaluated the test he will either recommend or not recommend the applicant for the position. The applicant who is recommended may also be told that if there is a loss of money or merchandise,

---

[1] John E. Reid and Associates have developed the "honesty evaluator," designed only for job applicants. This Reid Report consists of 158 questions, 42 similar to those found on standard applications, 116 key questions which are evaluated for "honesty tendencies." Thousands of tests over an eight year development period have proved the accuracy of judgments derived from it. "Our experience in conducting personnel examinations for more than 800 firms, ————, convinces us that there is no substitute either in accounting methods or various kinds of employe supervision, for proper personnel selection as a safeguard against employe dishonesty."

after he is employed, he may be asked to submit to a lie-detector examination.

Occasionally a company may be reluctant to communicate defections of a former employe. In Illinois proving the truth of the essentials of a defamatory communication is a complete defense if the communication was made "with good motives and for justifiable ends."[2]

Protecting a fellow merchant from loss at the hands of a dishonest employe would undoubtedly justify answering a request for information about an ex-employe applying for work. The courts in Illinois have found for the defendant in libel suits where it was proven that information was given in good faith. In one case the finding was for the plaintiff for reason of personal malice in a false report by one of the defendant's investigators.

An Oregon case involved copies of a photograph of plaintiff, taken and erroneously labeled "check artist" by the police department, and given to the Spokane Chamber of Commerce for distribution to its merchant members. Defendant retail store displayed its copy of the photograph in an employe restroom, together with pictures of shoplifters, forgers, and the like. Plaintiff sued the store for libel. Judgment for defendant was affirmed, on appeal, on the theory that reliance on the police label was sufficient to disprove the charge of malice, and that posting in a place used only by employes of the store was not such wide publication as to be an abuse of the privilege.

The extent of an investigation of a check being cashed may only include questioning, and examination of identification presented. This is done to determine that the person cashing the check is rightly in possession of it and that he can be located if the check is not honored by the bank.

Investigation of applicants for credit are of consequence in preventing loss because of bad risks and frauds. This is usually handled entirely by the credit department. The problem of apprehending persons making fraudulent purchases on genuine charge accounts is solved in cooperation with the protection department.

A person who is successful in charging merchandise fraudu-

[2] Ill. Const. Art. 2, par. 4.

lently at one time, like other criminals, will often repeat a pattern. The investigation of details of the fraudulent charges and the questioning of the customers and salespeople are important factors leading to the identification and capture of the purchaser.

One woman used stolen identification plates to purchase merchandise on five accounts, over a period of thirteen months.

Account A was used on ten different days during December, January and February. Account B was used on three days in January, February, and March; C was used for nineteen purchases on one day in March; D was used in June and September for a total of thirty-four purchases; E was used the next December.

Descriptions of the purchaser and an analysis of the purchases both indicated that the accounts were being used by one person.

Purchases were: women's, men's, and infants' wear—sizes typical on all accounts; jewelry, cosmetics, and other items; but unusual purchases on all accounts were yard goods, patterns, luncheons, and bakery goods.

Salespeople were found who were certain that they could identify the purchaser. The customers, who reported the fraudulent purchases, were interviewed for information which might be helpful. Customers B and D reported a suspect after they happened to discuss charge accounts at a social gathering and compared notes on their experiences. Upon further inquiry we learned that the suspect knew and had access to the homes of A and C.

Salespeople were taken to the neighborhood of the suspected purchaser, but were unable to see her, and because of the prominence of her family, we decided it would be advisable to apprehend her while making the false representation. Fraudulent purchases were reported on another account before she was caught.

Purchases were reported on account E by a school teacher. She remembered another teacher had seen our suspect come from her schoolroom one day when there was an alumni meeting in the school; also money was missing from her desk the same day.

The teacher secured a graduation photograph of the suspect which, although several years old, was identified by several of our salespeople.

In order to be positive of the identification, before going to court to request an arrest warrant, we arranged for several of our witnesses to attend an alumni dance at the school. The suspect was identified beyond any question of doubt and the investigation was successfully completed.

The owner or occupant of a building used as a store is not an insurer of the safety of his customer or other invitee while in the building. He may be liable for injuries sustained in an accident if he has been negligent and failed to exercise reasonable care for the safety of his customers.

Public liability insurance only protects for liability. It does not prevent a person from making a claim for non-liability injuries; therefore, each accident must be investigated. Some persons are prone to exaggerate the extent of their injuries arising from accidents and some will "dress up" the existing conditions in order to prove negligence. Just claims should be settled promptly. Unjust claims should be refused. Refusal to settle may lead to a lawsuit and the trial of a lawsuit begins with the investigation.

The purpose of the investigation is to carefully marshal all the facts promptly and efficiently, so that an accurate picture can be presented to the jury if the claim reaches litigation.

A person suffering injury from an accident should be taken care of immediately, but at the same time the condition of the property can be observed. Witnesses should be obtained and, in a store, they can be employes. The first statement that is made regarding the cause of the accident is usually the most accurate that can be obtained.

All the facts should be determined, as soon as possible, after the injured has been cared for. The investigator should make a written statement of the facts and conditions, including the date and time. Witnesses should be requested to sign the statements that they make. They can be used to refresh the memory, at a later date, if there is litigation. Photographs of the conditions found can be helpful.

Any further investigation will probably be handled or directed by the store's legal representative or the insurance company.

The importance of accident investigation cannot be over emphasized.

"Convict Two of Fraud on Store." A Chicago newspaper announced the results of another investigation in which a photograph played a prominent part.

The article explained that the two women, who had been intimate friends for many years, were charged with conspiracy to defraud the company of $3,500 by means of a fake personal injury suit.

During a civil suit for personal injury, brought by a woman who claimed to have broken her wrist in a fall, a surprise witness turned up to corroborate her account of the accident. There were no other witnesses and this one testified she had never seen the plaintiff before the day of the accident.

The jury believed the plaintiff and her witness because they returned a verdict in her favor. The defense attorney doubted their veracity.

The witness had testified that she managed an apartment building. That night an investigator and his wife called at her address to inquire for an apartment. When the woman explained the reason for keeping the couple waiting, she gave information that prompted further research. She stated that she had just returned home after being in court all day to testify for a *friend* of hers, and was changing her clothes.

The statement in itself was not sufficient information to take to the state's attorney. How could it be proven? Upon further inquiry it was learned that a daughter of the plaintiff had married prior to the alleged accident. It was also learned that a neighborhood newspaper had taken photographs of the wedding party. When a photograph was obtained that pictured "the surprise witness" in the wedding party with the plaintiff, we had enough material to take to the state's attorney. His office continued the investigation, secured further information and witnesses to convict the two women for fraud.

A liberal refund policy encourages thefts by the public and employes, and fraudulent charge purchases, in order to obtain cash refunds. Some customers will take advantage of the liberal policy by returning merchandise purchased from other sources. A fictitious name and address is often given on fraudulent refunds.

Some stores investigate refunds by intermittently sending letters requesting the reason for returns. A careful study of refunds may uncover loss factors.

Employes have been involved in fabulous fake refund schemes, in all parts of the country. An employe may admit deception on refunds, or to thefts, but from that point on, the work of the investigator has just started. Interrogation can help develop the pattern used and examination of records can prove up the extent of the loss. There may be a pattern in the use of names, addresses, merchandise, or amounts. One employe only wrote fictitious refunds for dictionaries and bibles. They were cashed by different cashiers throughout the store.

The process of elimination will vary in form according to the characteristics of any particular case which is being investigated.

In one case, the cash losses from common drawer cash registers amounted to $3,000 within a six months' period.

The investigation was started as soon as losses were reported and before a pattern had been established. The first, and natural action, was to request the shoppers to concentrate their test shopping on the salespeople working in the area. There were no results and the losses continued.

The next phase of the investigation was to study the backgrounds of the personnel having access to the registers involved. A saleslady was a logical prospect but close observation of her actions brought no results even though she worked every day losses occurred. She had a full time position elsewhere and had taken a part time job in order to help pay off some doctor bills. When she resigned, the losses stopped in her register and started in another one.

When the pattern of loss was finally established, from $20 to $100 disappeared at a time, but always on one of two days a week. A further check of the time records showed that a supervisor had worked every day that the losses had occurred. On the same two days of the week he had an assignment to collect the cash receipts from the registers, in a group of sections where the losses occurred.

The supervisor took a one week vacation—no losses. Arrangements were made to check him when he returned. Money was prepared to substitute in two registers. At closing time on his collection day he was called away, and kept busy, while the counted money was exchanged for the day's receipts. When the money was turned in to the cashier one register was short $60. When questioned the supervisor admitted all the thefts.

Another investigation of a series of $10 and $20 shortages in cashier inspector's receipts revealed that all the cashiers had worked on one floor of the store the days shortages occurred. The elimination of persons having contacts with the cashiers, and a check of time records, left only one suspect, a merchandise collector. By careful watching, the suspect was caught slipping a bill out of the cash drawer while picking up packages to be delivered.

Investigation of shrinkage will reveal errors as well as thefts. Costume jewelry is normally one of the higher shrinkage sections. Much of the loss is due to pilferage but careful checking of the pricing indicated carelessness in the marking room. Earrings were marked $3 a pair, should have been $4; a pin marked $3 should have been $5. A $30 necklace was incorrectly marked at $10. Errors discovered during a short period of investigation caused the buyer to have the prices verified on all her merchandise before placing it in stock.

In contrast to the costume jewelry section, all the dresses received in one section were properly marked and all the items purchased were received on the selling floor. The investigation of the dress section was due to a shrinkage of more than four per cent for one year. The section shrinkage had been consistently under one per cent for a number of years previously.

Assignment of detectives to the section ruled out shoplifting as the cause of shrinkage, and checkers' records accounted for all merchandise taken into the fitting rooms.

In order to eliminate the possibility of night losses a piece count of the garments was made daily, just after the store closed and just prior to opening. During one month there were no night losses, yet each day from two to fifteen garments were short on the count. A total of 159 garments were lost during the month, but detectives saw nothing stolen.

The manager of the section had turned down a suggestion that the garments being shown by salespeople be checked in and out of the stockroom, insisting that it couldn't be done. In desperation she agreed to an attempt at checking the stockroom. A system to check from the stockroom, instead of at the fitting rooms, was installed and the loss for the following month was only three garments, two of them from a reduced rack on the selling floor.

What had happened? The process of elimination convinced us that some employe had been stealing from the stockroom.

A survey of the personnel records showed that two saleswomen had been hired in one week at about the time the shrinkage jumped. They had both worked in a dress section of another store and the references for both were identical, "Services satisfactory—reduction in force." The period being post war, when no stores were reducing the force, the protection manager of the competitor store was consulted.

The other store had experienced excessive shortages in the section where the two salesladies had worked. Protection had become suspicious of the two, yet were unable to catch them stealing, so had requested their release. The large losses stopped.

After their release from our store, the shrinkage for a number of successive inventory periods was less than one-half the percentage they had been prior to the large increase.

This and other experiences were conclusive proof that a thorough investigation of shrinkage, with cooperation of the section supervisory group, will reduce shrinkage.

A "top-notch" store investigator should be affable; have the art of asking questions; be a good listener; then listen "between the lines." He should be diligent in his effort or search to discover relevant circumstances and should be able to analyze and catalogue facts and clues, so they can be used to advantage in the apprehension of criminals or reduction of shrinkage. Investigation is a science, and as such, good investigators merit consideration.

Chapter 24
GOAL FOR SHRINKAGE REDUCTION

A GOOD approach to a shrinkage reduction program is to establish a goal. Next, a program aimed at accomplishing the established goal should be planned and it should start at the management level. The program should be participated in by all divisions of the business, management, protection, accounting, personnel, merchandising, and service.

A review of systems should be made to determine if there are adequate controls and if they are satisfactorily enforced.

Does the store have definite and clearly stated rules designed to eliminate temptation which may lead to employe delinquency? Have the employes been informed of the penalty for violation of these rules? Employe rules should include: a pass-out procedure which applies to all and prohibits packages being kept in work areas where merchandise is stocked; all persons should be forbidden to record the sale for a personal purchase, wrap, rewrap, or apply a pass-out to his own package.

Lockers or a cloak room with security for purses and personal valuables should be available for all employes working with merchandise.

All systems, procedures, and rules should be consistently and fairly enforced for all personnel. Is it being done? The conscientious employe does not object to following rules that others adhere to but does resent restrictions that others can by-pass. It is extremely important to arrange a continuous check on enforcement of rules.

Review the shrinkage history for all sections. Compare the results with other comparable sections, the store average, or national or competitors' experience, and if a section has a shrinkage that is bad or too good, the section manager should be required to give an explanation and suggestions for improvement. Independent investigations should be made by the accounting or inventory control division and by protection.

If all applicants are well screened before hiring and are then placed in jobs for which they are suited, the company has a duty to instruct each one in his responsibility for protection and to encourage participation in loss prevention and shrinkage reduction.

All employes should be trained and retrained. Periodic, planned publicity should be practiced, reminding all employes of their responsibility for participation in the program. Protection should be explained in the initial training; the supervisor should review it; and the Protection Department should issue reminders at the most opportune times.

Shrinkage reduction can be effected by the assignment of an individual to an investigation of a section suffering poor inventory results. By following the movement of stock from the time it is received until it arrives in the section, and by asking questions of each person who comes in contact with the merchandise or the records, carelessness will be eliminated, and the following inventory will show an improvement.

At times the investigator may uncover various reasons for shrinkage; other times nothing tangible will be found; yet an improvement should result. No doubt the real reason for improvement is that all personnel, including supervisors, make a concentrated effort to be accurate, and watch merchandise and records more carefully, due to their interest in the investigation.

A survey of the kinds of merchandise shoplifted, from the "Cameron Study," might help to establish a goal for shrinkage reduction by pointing out the areas most vulnerable to shoplifting.

I have had discussions, with persons from many stores, regarding the value of fitting room checkers. I am convinced that they can more than pay their way and I think the "Cameron Study" supports my contention.

Women's clothing shoplifted by women, from an examination of 890 cases in the Women's Court of Chicago, on the complaints of thirteen department stores and shops, were as follows:

    11.8 per cent stole women's coats—suits, only
    4.9 per cent were from stores using checkers.

Goal for Shrinkage Reduction

26.4 per cent stole women's dresses, only 8.8 per cent were from stores using checkers.

The comparison in favor of checkers might have been greater if the total arrests, including those not prosecuted, of the thirteen stores were available. Many of them did not have checkers, and there is a certainty that not all women who shoplifted women's clothing, from the thirteen stores, were prosecuted.

Checkers are recommended, not only for protection, but also for the service they can render to customers and salespeople. A system for supplying name cards to the customers can assist the checker to summon the saleslady at anytime the customer wishes.

KINDS OF MERCHANDISE SHOPLIFTED
1000 STORE CASES

	Men %	Women %	Boys %	Girls %
Women's Suits-Coats	.0	4.9	.0	4.3
Women's Dresses	.7	8.8	.0	8.7
Women's Clothing, other	4.1	13.5	.0	2.9
Dress Accessories	14.3	29.1	8.8	15.2
Men's Suits	12.2	.3	.6	.0
Men's Clothing, other	8.8	1.0	.6	.0
Children's Clothing	1.4	7.3	4.4	2.2
Hats	.7	5.8	1.9	1.4
Purses	1.4	10.3	.0	2.2
Bill Folds, etc.	18.4	12.4	18.8	25.4
Jewelry	3.4	28.2	12.6	45.6
Cosmetics	1.4	5.8	.6	7.9
Toys	.7	1.6	15.7	2.2
China, Bric-a-brac	2.7	6.3	.6	2.2
Household	.7	4.7	.0	1.4
Books—Records	10.0	6.8	11.3	3.6
Stationery—cards	2.1	6.1	5.7	4.3
Umbrellas	1.4	1.8	.0	.0
Shoes—slippers	.7	1.4	.6	.7
Notions	.0	4.2	.6	.0
Remnants	.7	1.6	.0	.0
Food	1.4	2.9	1.3	.0
Brief cases—suitcases etc., over $10.00	12.9	.8	1.9	.7
Gadgets—over $10.00	8.2	6.5	32.1	5.8

Total percentages do not add to 100% because one person often steals more than one item.

196   *Shoplifting and Shrinkage Protection*

CHART NO. I

SHOPLIFTING ARRESTS BY MONTH—STORE CASES

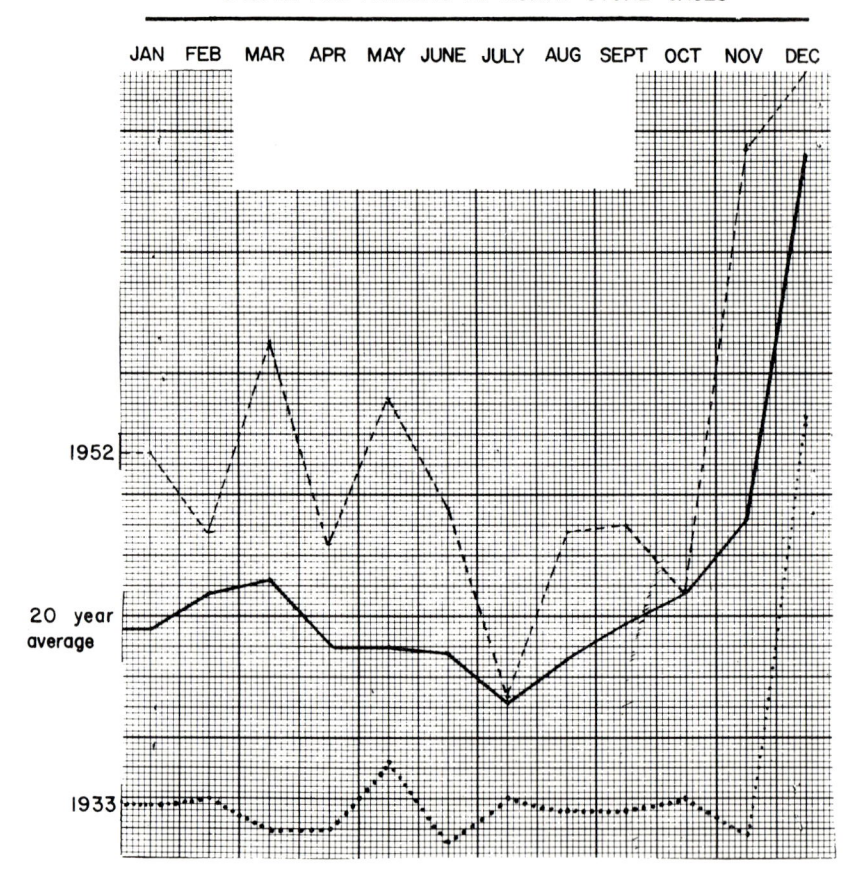

More amateur shoplifters are arrested with typical gift items just prior to Easter, Mother's Day and Christmas.

Chart number 1 indicates the periods in the year when shoplifting is most prevalent, and chart number 2 shows the times of the day when most arrests were made. They may be helpful in planning protection.

Goal for Shrinkage Reduction

CHART NO. 2

TIME OF THE DAY SHOPLIFTERS WERE ARRESTED

Approximately 700 cases

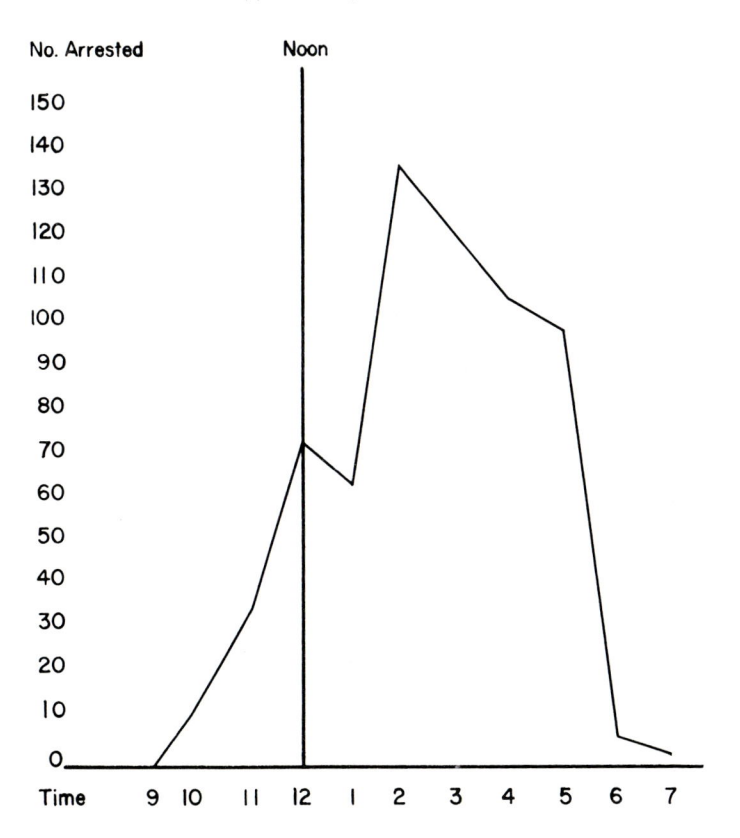

Chapter 25

TRAINING SUPERVISORS IN STORE PROTECTION

YOU MAY think that the problem of security and the need for training employes applies only to stores with several thousand employes and hundreds of thousands of customers each year, but that is not so. Stores that are owner operated or that have a half dozen employes are exposed to the same risks.

Several years ago we apprehended an old time shoplifter just before Easter, a friendly soul with whom I was well acquainted. She made bond at the detective bureau and, as is customary with many shoplifters, asked for a continuance when her case came up for hearing. She wanted a continuance for so-called professional reasons, that is to raise the fee for her defense lawyer. While out on bond, I received a very beautiful Easter greeting card from her and my immediate reaction was, "I wonder from what neighborhood shop this card was pilfered?"

The ambition of shoplifters know no bounds or I might explain further; a shoplifter may be crazy enough to steal a tray full of watches or a couple tomatoes. Several years ago our watch section reported that a man stepped behind the counter, opened a case and removed a tray of watches. He was leaving the store before anyone realized what had happened and then he ran or was lost in the crowd. We did not get him. Of course, we now have gates to the aisle in back of the watch counter and new locks on the cases. When we later learned watches were being peddled in near-by taverns and restaurants, we were able to identify them and have the man, who had stolen them, arrested and sent to the House of Correction. The following year an intruder in one of our kitchens proved to be the same man and he had stolen two tomatoes. After his arrest, the manner in which he held his coat sleeve in the palm of his hand was reason to investigate. When the sleeve was pulled up a wound on his wrist was revealed. He then explained he had been in an argument, decided to commit suicide, cut his wrist, walked toward the loop expecting to drop dead but when he arrived downtown decided he was hungry and wanted to live. So he went to get something to eat. He was committed to a mental institution for one of his later arrests. Crimes are committed against merchants by persons of both sexes, of all ages, races, and social and cultural groups.

We cannot educate all criminals so that they will not violate the law, but we can help our employes to learn how to minimize our losses.

Why do we train employes? It is good policy to provide training at all levels with the aim of securing and maintaining maximum effectiveness of all employes. And, every supervisor is responsible for the continuous training of all persons under his direction.

Why do I recommend that all employes be trained in Store Protection? Probably because of my own personal experience. While learning about protection myself, I could readily realize the great potentiality in training employes in protection.

> Every child capable of learning inevitably assimilates knowledge regarding property rights and thefts in the simpler situations. It is probably for this reason that everyone is somewhat criminal. College students, with few exceptions, doubtless due to poor memories, report an average of eight thefts or series of thefts between the age of seven, and continued in most cases to the age at which the reports were made.[1]

If there is any basis for this theory it would justify a training program.

Experience has proven that some employes succumb to temptation, and some employes were dishonest by choice. We know that a theft requires a desire for the results to be secured, accompanied by the minimum danger of detection and punishment. Training for protection not only points out the action of shoplifters, because knowing shoplifters' methods may reduce "take-withs," but it also stresses the importance of employes adhering to rules which are designed to help prevent temptation.

[1] Sutherland, Edwin H.: *Principles of Criminology*, 3rd Edition, J. B. Lippincott Company, Publisher, Chicago, Philadelphia, New York, 1939, p. 5.

"crime is not a problem that solely concerns the mayor, the chief of police and the criminal courts of a city. The problem of crime lies squarely in the laps of the people who work in this and every other business—and who derive their livelihood from the store and from this city. Thus, crime and its cure is our problem, at home, in the schools and where we work."

One of the first programs we presented to supervisors was dubbed "The Medicine Show," because picture posters, and actual booster equipment, which had been used by shoplifters, was demonstrated. The success of that effort prompted the development of a moving picture for the supervisory group.

As a prelude to the picture we said, "We do not know what per cent of our employes fall in the group that remains honest because of supervision and the efficiency of the systems, but we do know there is a sufficient number to warrant the training of all employes to think in terms of theft prevention, not only when dealing with the public, but also in their own actions."

It is necessary to train everyone—

The Stock Boy, when asked why he allowed other employes to steal cleansing tissues from his stock truck while in transit, one said, "when I objected, the girls told me that the stock boys before me had allowed them to do it, and I didn't want to be a rat. I did tell the man in the stockroom to put them on the bottom of the truck with the bigger things on top, so they couldn't get them."

The Salesperson, who should realize that in addition to protecting merchandise, it is absolutely essential that salescheck arithmetic be accurate; measurements, weights, and counts be exact; and every sale be properly recorded with a copy of the salescheck delivered to the customer.

The Supervisor, who has a duty to set an example and enforce adherence by all employes to company rules which have been established to help prevent temptation.

This program again reviewed rules and procedures and pictured actual methods used by both shoplifters and employes in committing thefts.

We also quoted comments of employes who had been apprehended such as: one stock boy, who had been apprehended, reasoned that if his boss could get away with taking packages out without a pass-out, he could too.

Several years later we again produced moving pictures, one for supervisors, still stressing the need for systems and rules, and the need for enforcing them, again citing case histories to overcome any doubts. The other picture was shown to all employes. The introduction was posed for and narrated by our General Merchandise Manager, a Vice-President of the company, which indicated the cooperation given the program by management. His comments explain the nature of the picture:

> ... the members of our Protection Department have prepared this film to help us all guard against one of the things that may harm our reputation. This is a problem common to all stores.
>
> It is the problem of Inventory Shrinkage, which is our way of describing the ways by which store merchandise or money are lost, strayed, or stolen, and when that happens it concerns us all—not only in our reputation but in our pocketbooks. For the amount of such losses in any single month reaches a substantial total.

The picture demonstrated some shoplifters' actions, also the best methods for handling merchandise and cash, and was summarized as follows:

Theft can be prevented by
    Alertness
    Observation, and
    Cooperation with Protection
Errors can be prevented by care in
    Figuring
    Counting
    Weighing
    Measuring
Reports for mark downs should be made for
    Loss
    Breakage
    Damage
Make each sale at
    Correct Retail, or
    Record the Discount

Give a customer's memorandum with every purchase
Guard company and your personal cash
Adhere to Employes rules

Brochures were given to everyone attending the movie showings. One, "To All Employes," was primarily a reminder of rules and procedures; the other, "Hints to Supervisors for Reducing Shrinkage," emphasized supervisory responsibilities.

You are correct if you think at this point, that I have been repeating. I have. These, and many other methods have been used in training employes. Training and retraining for store protection is a never ending duty because the time will probably never come when merchants do not suffer loss.

May I suggest at this point that the store owner who is at one time, the Board of Directors, the Executive, and the Supervisor, can benefit by placing emphasis on security even though his organization is not large enough to warrant a formal training program.

There are several reasons why I emphasize the training of supervisors in shrinkage reduction:

First—the supervisor is responsible for the satisfactory results of his department and shrinkage affects profits adversely.

Second—probably the major part of his training for his responsibilities has been in fields other than protection. Protection is more or less of a side line to the merchant who devotes his time to the latest in fashion, buying, planning, promoting, and personnel.

Third—he is responsible for the employes he supervises, and because of daily contacts with them, he can do more than anyone else to train them. Also, the example that he sets means so much, especially in the retail business.

Because many merchants are not trained in protection problems, some are inclined to take a trivial view of the annual shrinkage figure. It is easy to assume that the figure is incorrect and the result of accounting errors.

The stinging remark attributed to the manager of a large store and published in a trade paper explains the attitude of some supervisors; "any store manager who believes his loss figure is not reasonably accurate and is mainly a result of bookkeeping errors, should either change his system or change his executives."

Altering Supervision. Of equal importance to theft prevention is an alert supervisory force. Without it, no theft prevention measures will be really effective. Companies report the use of foreman meetings as an effective way to alert supervisors to the problem of reducing thefts.[2]

Poor theft control is an indication of lax management that may show up in loose inventory control, ...

Stopping stealing boils down to just another management problem. It should be treated as such.[3]

Supervisors know that diamonds, guns, furs, and other types of value merchandise must be kept locked and under cover, and only shown in numbers of units that can be easily protected.

They should be alerted that better apparel and accessories are particularly tempting to the professional shoplifters, because of a ready market and high resale value.

The fitting room method of selling creates a haven for the professional, as well as the casual shoplifter, who allows her desire to conquer her conscience.

Special care should be exercised in protecting at least the upper half price range of any section merchandise, as experience has proven it the most vulnerable. Extra special care should be given to luxury items, such as a $350 handkerchief, $250 hats, and $165 purses, or $750 top coats, because investigation of loss usually reveals negligent handling.

Initial training can lay the ground work for protection, but there must be follow-up by the supervisor to make it effective. For example, a $350 handkerchief disappeared. A salesperson remembered showing the expensive handkerchiefs to two men. She did not remember if the handkerchief was in the box when she showed it, nor whether or not she left the box on the counter for any length of time. In all probability that was the time that the handkerchief disappeared, but unless she was trained, and retrained, to think of protecting her stock, she cannot be criticized.

The average unit price of handkerchiefs is seventy-five cents to one dollar each. A loss of 350 of the average price articles would

[2] *Industrial Security III.* Theft Control Procedures. Studies in Business Policy. No. 70, National Industrial Conference Board, Inc., New York, p. 7.

[3] Stop the Thief in Your Plant. *Factory Management and Maintenance.* Volume 112, Number 9, McGraw-Hill Publication. p. 85.

cause no greater shrinkage than the loss of the one luxury item. What can be done? An inventory may show that there are only a few pieces priced at $10 to $350 each. Special training should be given in the section to teach respect for the value of the expensive articles.

Locking them up, nights at least, would create a good effect. A running inventory with regular physical counts of the expensive items would help to impress the salespeople with their value. A real appreciation of the value might also help the employe build up a greater selling interest in the items.

The store owner, or section supervisor, who takes a personal concern of loss and shrinkage, and recognizes the possible risks, can induce participation of both employes and protection agents in loss prevention.

Chapter 26

REWARDS AND TRAINING EMPLOYES FOR PROTECTION

IN THE interest of the welfare of his employer, or his company, every loyal employe should report any knowledge he may have regarding any person stealing from the company. A reward policy for stores will encourage employes to be alert and watchful, and to report suspicions.

It is not difficult to gain the cooperation of most employes in reporting shoplifters but many are reluctant to report a fellow employe. But invariably after an employe has been apprehended stealing, other employes will report additional information, either of known thefts by the individual or suspicions of his actions. This information is usually received after the case has been disposed of, and too late to be helpful.

It is not unusual for rewards to be offered for information leading to the detection or capture of a criminal, or the recovery of lost or stolen property.

Research indicates that rewards to employes responsible for information, leading to arrests, were paid by stores as far back as 1895. I have recommended to other stores that they institute the Reward Policy, and they have indicated successful results from the application of it.

Some employes will never recognize a wrong action regardless of the training received. One old time professional shoplifter commented, "Some salespeople are so dumb you can steal right under their noses; all they are interested in are sales." Other employes have a natural talent for spotting crime and are diplomatic enough to conceal their own astonishment until they can get help. A reward should not be paid to untrained employes who take action themselves and make an arrest.

Sometimes more than one person will report on the same actions. Care should be used in determining the first informant and there are occasions when it may be necessary to reward more than one person for the same information. If two have cooperated and think that the reward should be divided, they should determine the split.

Occasionally a cleaner or other employe will find company money or valuables, sometimes in a substantial amount and turn it in. It is a good policy to pay the finder a reward, possibly 10 per cent.

An informant should not have to ask for his reward; if he does, some of the benefit of the program will be lost. It should be paid promptly and appreciation extended to the recipient for his alertness.

The Reward Program should be given publicity. It can be stated in various forms, in notices, in company publications, and by posters displayed in employe only areas. Reward publicity might also be a deterring factor to some easily tempted persons.

A notice that I have used announced: "REWARD . . . for the detection of theft . . . for information leading to the apprehension by PROTECTION of persons stealing from your Company—shoplifting—stockroom thefts—thefts of money—fraudulent charge purchases—fraudulent refunds and credits. DO NOT take action yourself or personally accuse anyone, DO CALL ———, or tell your Floor Manager or Section Manager, who will call a Special Operator. You will be paid a reward based on the value of Company property recovered. Recovery . . . , Your Reward. . . ."

Rewards for sums of several hundred dollars have been paid when employes have given information that led to a substantial recovery. The publicized amount might range from $5 to $25 based on the value of the recovery.

There are two methods for reducing losses. One is to prevent thefts, the other is to apprehend thieves. If a store has a protection department that is responsible for arrests, it is advisable to apprehend the shoplifters. Store employes can prevent losses by being attentive to the public, or they can assist protection in making arrests by information and diplomatic actions.

Employes should be trained in what action to take when they are suspicious of a person shoplifting. If the store maintains a protection department, all employes should be aware of it and instructed how to report a suspicion. They should also be instructed to proceed with their own duties after their suspicion has been reported to an operator and not allow their personal interest in the proceedings to interfere with the operator's work.

If the store does not have a protection department, arrangements may be made to report suspicions to a manager or some other individual. When no help is available an offer to be helpful or to serve the suspected may prevent a loss.

The policy practiced by the personnel of some shops, especially those belonging to some chains, is a deterrent to shoplifters. If a salesman is busy at the time another customer enters the store, a greeting and the comment, "I will be with you soon," or "please be seated," can cause a booster to go on his way. The legitimate customer is usually pleased to be greeted and to have his presence recognized.

Salespeople, like detectives, are not always aware of the specific actions that arouse their suspicion. A shoplifter cannot be identified by appearance unless he is known. Yet a salesman phoned protection because, to him, a man looked wrong. The man did place five phonograph records under his arm, under his top coat.

It is surprising to learn of the stupidity of some people. A saleswoman told a fellow employe that she was going to wear a sweater out of the store as she removed all identification tags from it. The loyal employe could do only one thing and that was to report the conversation to her supervisor.

Circumstances vary and every case is different, yet examples of cases should be helpful in training programs.

From time to time, the owners or managers of shops or small stores, that do not have a protection department, have asked for advice in loss prevention. My advice is to learn first some of the tactics of shoplifters, then train all personnel. The experience of one small suburban store will show what can be done.

Shrinkage in this store had been no problem for years. Suddenly the manager realized that they were suffering substantial losses. The following items were missing: two suits at $155 each, and one at $125, three blouses at $10.95 each, one compact $15, and one dress $69.75.

The personnel of the store proved to be apt pupils and learned to watch for situations they had not previously suspected. Their alertness soon paid off.

One couple, a woman and a man, and two other men entered the store—strangers—who obviously did not belong in that area. Because the personnel watched them closely, they soon realized they were in the wrong place and left the store. An employe followed and saw these strangers meet at a parked car.

A check of the Bureau of Identification records revealed that the man to whom the auto license was issued had a long police record, including shoplifting.

The losses stopped. Since then the store has had several other cases in which they feel sure that they prevented loss.

The moral of this story is that people in this store learned what to watch for in the actions of shoplifters, and also that much courteous attention will usually discourage a thief.

A university student employed as a part time clerk in a suburban jewelry store might have prevented the loss of a tray of rings valued at $2,500.

A man entered the jewelry store, at noon, while the saleslady was alone, and asked to see diamond rings.

He said the rings she showed him were not good enough and asked to look at one that was displayed in the window. The newspaper account states that the clerk left several trays of rings on the counter while she went to the window. When she returned the man said he would go to his car and bring his wife to make the selection. The clerk noticed too late that a tray of rings was missing.

The saleslady should not be censured unless she had been trained in safe methods for displaying valuables. It should not be necessary to show several trays of diamond rings at one time. The request to see one from the window should have been a warning to replace the "not good enough" rings in the case. If reasonable care had been practiced a Chicago newspaper would have been minus one article, "CLERK SHOWS HIM JEWELRY AND TURNS BACK."

The professional shoplifter who remarked that she could steal from under the noses of some salespeople, because they are interested only in sales, no doubt, had studied the selling habits of many. Sales training should be supplemented with protection training to prevent loss and increase profit.

The "Cameron Study" found that tips from store personnel resulted in the arrest of shoplifters as follows:

Shoplifters	Number of Tips	Per Cent	Total Survey Cases
Men	36	24.5	147
Boys	25	15.7	159
Women	70	9.9	709
Girls	10	7.2	138
Total	141	12.2	1153

The fact that store personnel first suspected 12.2 per cent of 1,153 shoplifters arrested, over a period of time, is justification for a reward system and training for protection. If a store does not have persons authorized to make arrests, vigilance of employes may prevent loss.

About 11:00 a.m., a woman, carrying an empty bag, appeared to be trying to steal a blouse. She circled the room several times and each time tried to take the blouse. It appeared that she lost her nerve and left the store, but she appeared again about 1:00 p.m. This time she was followed until she removed a bottle of cologne from the counter and folded an empty bag around it before leaving. She carried other stolen merchandise at the time.

While walking through a dress section, a detective saw a woman standing before a mirror with several dresses over her arm and holding a large open paper bag. Full price tickets, indicating that they had not been sold, were visible. She folded one dress and placed it in the bag. After placing the other dresses on a rack, she was followed and arrested when she stole another article.

A woman carrying a brown paper shopping bag was watched. When she picked up an article from a counter, she would step in back of another customer to conceal the article in the shopping bag.

An operator watched a woman, who carried a shopping bag, remove a sweater from a counter and fold it over several times. The operator could not get close enough to her to see her place it in the bag, but was sure from her actions that she had done so. She was followed to a wash room where she entered a toilet booth, and by standing on the adjoining toilet, the operator saw the shoplifter take the sweater from the bag, remove the price ticket, and put the sweater on.

The way a woman held her right arm and the motion of her left arm reaching under her coat to the right arm pit, caused a detective to think something was being carried there. This woman was followed and arrested after stealing bacon and canned chicken.

Two men carrying bad looking or booster bags appeared to be narcotic addicts and were followed. They were arrested, after boosting, and the surmise that they were addicts proved to be correct.

A man was seen to walk away from a display table. He seemed to be holding something in his left hand, which he held down and close to his body. He was followed and, as he walked along, he put something into his coat pocket. The operator watched for him to return. Several days later he came back, took a figure of a mule, and concealed it under his coat.

A woman was arrested because, when she was first noticed, she held her arm under a bulge in her coat at the left side waist line. She also stole a sweater and put it under her coat in the same place.

A young lady tried on coats, which were several sizes too large for her, over her heavy jacket. She refused the help of salespeople. She left the store and as she did she dropped small pieces of the price tag which she had removed from a coat. The operator returned to the coat section and was watching when the woman returned about one half hour later. She went directly to the rack, removed the coat from which she had previously taken the price tag, put it on, and walked out.

A stolen coat was recovered because a detective followed a woman who hurriedly left the coat section wearing a coat which looked like new merchandise. The woman looked around as she walked away and out of the store. She made the mistake of entering again, through another doorway, and stealing a diary, which she concealed between her purse and her arm.

It is not necessary for a detective to take a chance and make an arrest if not sure of the facts. Invariably the professional boosters will return to a good spot, and amateurs will usually do the same if they have been successful in previous thefts.

A detective saw a man standing before a shelf of fine glassware. When he left, one of a pair of bottles was missing. He looked around and returned to the shelf. When he left the second time, the second bottle was missing, but the detective had not been able to get in a position to see him take it or to see where it was concealed.

One evening, several weeks later, the same man walked through the glassware section, was followed, and arrested when he stole an expensive table scarf. He gave a written authorization to search his room and the previously stolen bottles were recovered, along with other stolen artwares.

One section had reported young men's suits and coats, all one size, were missing from stock. While watching the section, a young man was seen to enter just before closing time, remove a suit from the rack, go into a fitting room, wait until the section personnel had gone home, then leave with the suit. He was not considered to be a professional shoplifter, but often professionals are arrested because of losses being reported. Also, professionals have been arrested at, or right after, closing time.

A women's suit section had reported finding skirts rolled up and stuffed into the sleeves of jackets. By watching this area, a young woman narcotic addict was arrested. She would remove the skirt from the hanger, roll it up and place it in a sleeve, then walk around the rack, at the same time looking around the room. If the coast seemed clear, she would return and slip the jacket with the hanger under her coat. She then went to a telephone booth and put it in a suit box that she carried.

Occasionally a well known professional shoplifter can be followed and apprehended, as one was when a detective recognized her on the first floor. It is difficult though for an operator to recognize a professional and follow her without being seen.

One of the detectives reported repeatedly that a woman would immediately leave the floor, and the store, when they would meet. The detective did not know the woman but felt certain that she was a good booster. She was. The detective was instructed to sit in a buyer's office, at a telephone, until the woman was seen again and then phone the protection office.

During the second day of waiting, the woman appeared and a store detective, who knew most of the old time professionals, and two city detectives went to the floor. The woman was a notorious shoplifter, who had a long police record, but no recent arrests. She was brought to the office where all the protection personnel were able to see her. She was then put on notice that she would be arrested for trespassing at any future time she was seen in the store.

I referred to a survey that indicates that 12.6 per cent of those arrested used shopping bags, and 20 per cent used paper bags, to conceal stolen merchandise. The same survey indicated that 29 per cent of those arrested were first spotted because of nervous or furtive actions.

Detectives described some of these actions as follows:

"I noticed three boys as they hurried to the bathing suit counter. The way they looked around, as they handled the suits, caused me to watch them."

"I first noticed two women looking around as they stood close to a skirt rack. They later took skirts which were put under their coats."

"I noticed the woman because she was at the end of a counter, near a post, and looking around. She tried on a belt and left it on, then tried on other belts, taking them off, but always leaving the first one on. She left without paying for it and went through the store to take other items."

"I first saw this man at the wallet counter, looking around. He carried a newspaper and put the wallets between the pages."

"Standing near a door, about fifteen minutes before closing time, I noticed a woman enter the store and look around. She carried a plastic zipper bag and a typical 'booster' paper bag. She went directly to the sweater counter, picked one up, held it in front of herself concealed by the bag she carried, and left the store. She entered and left within just a few minutes."

"I saw this man carrying a shopping bag and walking around the toy department. He didn't look at anything except wrapping desks and the packages lying around them. He walked into another section and stopped at a truck full of packages, threw his coat over it, then picked up the coat and a package and walked up the stairs."

"I saw the woman looking at Christmas tree ornaments. She walked around the counter with one in her hand, then she looked around and put it in her pocket. She did this twice, then left the section, and I followed her. She returned to the ornament counter, picked up a box of ornaments, walked around the counter, and after looking all around, she slipped the box into her shopping bag. She left the section, then again returned, took more ornaments and put them in her other pocket. She went down a stairway and as she started to leave I apprehended her."

"I noticed a man in the woman's coat section, holding a coat on a hanger with both hands near the lapels, but he was looking around the section rather than at the coat. Then I recognized the overcoat that he wore as the same dirty tweed coat, with frayed pockets, that he wore another time I encountered him. That was months ago. He is the man who put on a $195 sports coat in the men's section and then started to put his overcoat on over it. Our eyes met and he quickly removed the coat, threw it, grabbed his coat, and ran." This time he was arrested after taking a woman's coat.

"I first noticed that he seemed nervous and kept looking around as if to see if anyone was after him. He also carried a bad bag so I watched him. The first thing he took was the sausage, which he put in the bag, then the other things."

"I saw this man make a nervous move, as though on guard; then he looked from side to side, before he took two pairs of pajamas, put them under his suit coat, and walked away."

"I saw the five boys looking around as if up to no good." One woman detective was able to round up the five and bring them to the protection office. One had tried to throw his loot over a stair railing. An authoritative command caused him to pick it up and bring it to the office.

"As I passed the counter, I saw the woman look slowly from side to side, while holding a string of beads. She put them in her paper bag so I followed her."

"This lady appeared very nervous as she walked up to the blouse counter. She selected a blouse, scooped it under her coat, and left."

"I saw this man looking at key cases. He acted kind of nervous. As I watched him he picked up a case, palmed it, then stepped behind some other people and put it in his pocket."

"This man was looking at lighters and at the same time looking around the section; also he was shabby and didn't look like a customer for that type of merchandise. He made a motion as though putting the lighter back. Instead he carried it away in his hand and then put it in his pocket."

"I saw the two boys fooling around the wallet counter. One boy picked up a wallet, looked around, then laid it down at the edge of the counter. He looked around again, picked it up and put it in the other boy's back pocket."

"The lady picked up a wallet at one end of the counter and walked toward the other end, at the same time looking all around. She stepped in back of another customer and placed it in her pocket."

"I noticed this woman at the jewelry counter. She had something behind her bag that looked like a card with earrings on it. As she left the section she looked around and put it in her bag so I followed her and saw her get the other merchandise."

"I saw the boy standing at the pipe counter, handling pipes and looking around. He put a pipe up his coat sleeve, then put his hand in his pocket and let the pipe slide into the pocket."

The story is usually the same; however, there are always variations, such as the following:

"I noticed the two young ladies sitting back to back in the sportswear section. The mouth of one moved as though she was talking to some one, but no one was around, except the girl behind her. The girl who had apparently been listening, got up quickly, walked behind a rack, removed a coat from a hanger, placed it over her arm and started to walk behind a counter. By this time the one who had moved her lips joined her with a large bag she had held in her lap. They looked around, rolled up the coat and stuffed it into the bag. They separated and I followed the one with the bag and the coat and stopped her."

Chapter 28

HOW SOME EMPLOYES HAVE SPOTTED THIEVES

THE SURVEY, previously mentioned, in which detectives spotted shoplifters because of bad bags 20 per cent and shopping bags 12.6 per cent, indicated that 29 per cent of the test group were first watched because of furtive or nervous actions. Store employes should be instructed regarding this trait of shoplifters.

The comments of one alert saleslady aptly describes the characteristic actions of many shoplifters. She was interviewed because of her success in recognizing the actions, and her ability to secure aid without alerting the booster:

> I have been successful because I study the habits of my customers and I have learned that the habits of shoplifters are not the same. I have noticed that a shoplifter may approach the counter slowly, and when I look will turn around and possibly walk away. She may return and fondle an article and hold it for a while, then drop it if someone approaches, but just before she is ready to take it, she will usually put her hand on the article and then give that "up look," and look all around before lifting it up.
>
> Once I recognize the actions of a shoplifter I never look directly at her but if I have a customer I will excuse myself and quietly ask a fellow employe to call protection, or I walk to the telephone and call for a detective.
>
> The person I suspect does not always steal. However, there is no harm done because I have not let it be known that I was suspicious. I try to remember the person I am suspicious of and anyone who may steal before I can call for a detective. Then the next time they come in, I phone at once.

This saleslady has done an excellent job of studying people and handling the situation quietly and diplomatically. One time a detective made an arrest of a person that he thought she had called him to watch previously. She did not remember the woman but said she might have called. "If I am suspicious of the movement of a person's hands, I never look into the face; I walk to the telephone. If that happened with this woman, I would not recognize her."

Other employes can help to spot the shoplifters who allow their actions to indicate their intent.

One salesman who has been responsible for shoplifters being apprehended is well aware of the trait. Three teen-age boys attracted his attention because they appeared nervous and were very shifty in manner. They later stole sweaters and neckties. He noticed that two men appeared furtive, nervous, and watchful, while picking new threads off a coat. Then he noticed that they looked out of place because they were unkempt. His call for aid was the reason that they were apprehended with two stolen coats, $100 each.

"She looked around for a moment." A shoplifter, arrested many times and well known to protection personnel, was again arrested for stealing four skeins of yarn and one package of bird cage liners. A saleswoman who was serving a customer saw the woman holding a skein of yarn in her hand:

> I happened to look up at her and as I did she walked around our table. She looked around for a moment and with that she tucked the yarn under her coat. I excused myself from my customer and asked our floorman to call protection, while I casually pretended I was looking for some merchandise. I kept track of her until an operator arrived; then I returned to my customer.

A saleswoman in the handkerchief section frequently spots shoplifters. When interviewed she explained that it is always the manner in which they handle the handkerchiefs that arouses the suspicions. This is another case of studying the actions of the customers.

> They will fold and stack them, one woman stacked thirty-seven before stealing, or they will bunch up the handkerchiefs while looking up and around.

A salesperson suspected a teen-age boy because he removed a fitted traveling case from a fixture to the floor and removed the price tag. A phone call to protection brought an operator who saw the boy straddle the case and inch it along the floor by shuffling his feet. He pushed the case along the floor, in this manner, for about 150 feet. There he quickly picked up the case and ran up the stairway to the first floor. The operator stopped him but he broke away and escaped. She recovered the case.

Purses equipped with a portable radio were priced complete, but the radios were kept in a drawer. The purses were displayed on the counter without the radio. The two were assembled when a sale was made. When a woman came to the counter, with one of the purses in a paper bag, and asked for a refund because her husband had paid too much for it, the salesperson stated that she would call for an adjuster. The customer did not wait; she went to a public telephone and gave the salesperson time to get a detective.

The woman next entered the lingerie department where she picked up a $50 night gown, asked to have it exchanged for one at $10.95 with the difference in cash, because her husband had paid too much for it.

A salesman in the hat section called for aid and a shoplifter was apprehended, because the shoplifter appeared so "arrogant." He attracted the salesman's attention because of his disregard of store property. He tried on many hats and left them lay where they fell on the counter, then left wearing one. Having worn none when he entered, the salesman followed the man but lost him in the crowd.

Later the salesman immediately phoned for aid when he saw the same man enter the suit section. The man was arrested for stealing a suit of clothes.

An interview with a saleslady:

> It was during the busy Christmas season that I first became aware of the woman. The first time I saw her I didn't give her a thought, but then she came in a few days later to return a pair of pajamas. She appeared to be honest enough, but appeared to be a little nervous and talked constantly about her sister buying these gifts for her son who wasn't pleased with the selection. I thought I would have to remember her.
>
> The third time I saw her was a week or two later. She was returning two shirts and I didn't know what to do so I gave her a refund.

Suggested Brochures and Reports   227

If a brochure is given to all employes, I would then recommend that one be prepared and given to all persons in a supervisory capacity. It would cover the same information plus additional suggestions for enforcement.

Such a brochure might be set up as follows:

HINTS TO SUPERVISORS FOR REDUCING SHRINKAGE

Enforcement of the following rules and procedures will help you reduce shrinkage. Periodic discussions during section meetings may help you gain the cooperation of your personnel in this effort.

"I never use a pass-out." Thefts of one employe who evaded the pass-out procedure by leaving the store during business hours.

Pass-Out Procedure—It is not uncommon for employes who have violated the "pass-out" procedure to claim lack of knowledge. Employes must not wrap, re-wrap, or re-apply "pass-outs" to their own packages.

Employes' "Own Goods Pass-Out" Procedure—Employes' "own goods" must be inspected and itemized on an "own goods pass-out." The pass-out must be signed and sent to a pass-out desk with the merchandise for wrapping and validation. Items purchased outside our store and accompanied by salescheck may be taken direct to pass-out desk.

Employes' Personal Packages—Personal packages must not be kept in merchandise areas. Employes are sometimes tempted to add section merchandise to packages kept in the section.

Employes' Purses—Purses must be kept in lockers, checkrooms, or other approved areas. This provides security for the owner, prevents temptation to purse thieves, and minimizes temptation for some employe to take section merchandise.

Coats and Hats—Coats and hats should be kept in lockers or checkrooms. This provides security for owners and protection for store merchandise. Watch especially your part-time workers, including stock boys, to see that clothing is not kept in stock rooms.

Disposal of "As Is" Merchandise and Discarded Equipment. Parts and Supplies—Strict adherence to the rules prevents temptation by making legitimate transactions and pass-out for all articles taken out of the store.

Saleschecks and Cash Register Receipts.—A record of sale must be issued and delivered to the customer with each sale. No employe is allowed to write saleschecks or ring up sales for own purchases.

Discount Sales—According to store procedure.

Own Goods Saleschecks—All merchandise to be sent out on an "own goods" shipper must be inspected by an authorized person, and this person must sign the shipper.

Markdowns—Markdowns must be recorded for theft, breakage, and damage, and thefts should be reported promptly.

Security of Valuable Merchandise, Day and Night—Valuable merchandise must always be protected, including sign ups in receiving and shipping. Protect valuable displays. Lock valuables at night. Lock stockrooms. Cover other merchandise to reduce temptation to night workers.

Check All Theft Possibilities—Shoplifting. Stockroom prowlers (restrict stockrooms to authorized personnel only). Fraudulent refunds and exchanges. Forged credits. Own goods shipments. Employe Larceny: Cash from sales. Merchandise from section. Merchandise from opening and marking rooms; stockrooms; warehouses; in transit to and from sections; packing rooms; manufacturers' returns; exchange; bale rooms and dummy elevators; workrooms. Giving of merchandise or special prices to friends.

Investigate All Unusual Occurrences—If in doubt, *Call Protection.* Spot check to determine if losses occur during or after business hours. Report suspicions promptly. A shopping service is available to detect dishonesty in sales transactions; or carelessness in counting, measuring, or weighing merchandise. Report any individual who persists in wrapping merchandise before recording the sale, or who fail to include a record of sale in the package.

Can you determine what portion of your section shrinkage was due to theft and the portion due to errors or carelessness?

Check for Errors in—Pricing of invoices. Counting of merchandise received. (Spot check counts in the selling section.) Marking. (Be sure the retail on both merchandise and invoice is identical.)

Check for Errors in—Salescheck arithmetic. Order filling. Handling of credits. (Be sure to record necessary markdowns.) Re-marking. Listing of section number on records. Transferring of merchandise; inter-store, inter-section, no charge. Price changes. Recording of markdowns for lost and damaged merchandise. Workroom charges. Inventory. Receiving of merchandise through unauthorized channels.

Check for Carelessness in—Taking price changes on damaged merchandise. Taking markdowns on adjustments and credits, including alterations or labor. Taking markdowns on stolen merchandise. Recording loans both customer and inter-section. Recording and controlling merchandise removed for showing or selling in other sections. Returning of merchandise on loan or checked out to other sections. Transporting of merchandise within the store. Physically protecting merchandise, displays, storing, covering, locking. Throwing away merchandise. Making transfer saleschecks. Inventory taking and records.

If you are not sure how to handle any records or inventory problems, ask the Merchandise Records and Inventory Control Office. Watch for completeness and accuracy.

Special reports distributed to supervisors at opportune times create interest and discussion. Examples of some that I have distributed:

PROTECTION REPORT #____

You were quoted shrinkage figures, covering a period of years, at the meeting "For Discussion of the Annual Inventory." This prompted us to analyze our records of arrests, to determine if we could throw some light on the part theft contributes to shrinkage.

The chart (page 196) may help in planning your shrinkage prevention program this year. It has been said that the "planets influence human actions." Perhaps this is not so, but we are convinced that the seasons are conducive to certain types of theft.

Fashion merchandise is always more tempting at the beginning of a season.

More persons are apprehended with typical gift items prior to Easter, Mother's Day, and Christmas.

The fact that the fewest number of persons are apprehended in mid-summer may be due to reduced traffic, but the reason probably is because fewer coats are worn, thereby making it more difficult to conceal stolen articles.

You will notice from the chart that the greatest number of arrests are made during the last two months of the year. Your greatest loss or shrinkage also occurs during that period.

You can help reduce your shrinkage, *at any time of the year*, by notifying Protection of any known losses or thefts, and by training section personnel to quietly and quickly phone, at any time a person is suspected of stealing.

Shrinkage prevention is the job of all employes and is a year round task.

Signed _____ Protection.

The following is another approach:

PROTECTION REPORT #____

May we relate the particulars of the plight of a long time employe, a current case. Some of the details may help to explain

Suggested Brochures and Reports

why you should help to enforce the "Pass-out" procedure and also aid in emphasizing the importance of adhering to the procedure on "Disposal of As Is Merchandise and Discarded Equipment, Parts, and Supplies." Both of these procedures were established to help prevent temptation and preclude employes getting into trouble.

About a week ago, an employe was observed, carrying packages from a merchandise section and handling them in a suspicious manner. A few days later the same individual was seen to put a garment into a bag, apply a register check to it and carry it out of the section with two other pass-out packages. We dislike for any employe to steal, but here was a person with many years of service with the company. Could we learn anything from her to prevent such occurrences in the future?

The merchandise, an $8.95 garment, was taken to give to a poor family. Much "As Is," old or discarded merchandise had previously been given to this person for the same family. The desire for her to give had been established. The register check she applied as a pass-out was one obtained from a twenty-one cent purchase in another section.

The opportunity was there because the person kept other packages in the section and had followed the practice of opening, combining and re-sealing personal packages. The only explanation for the action was, "I guess I have been here so long that I just ignore the rules."

Would more strict section enforcement of the Pass-Out rules have helped to prevent the occurrence?

We think the Company's policy as described in Procedure #_____ would assist in eliminating the idea of getting something for nothing. It is not uncommon for an employe to get the habit of taking "As Is or Damaged Merchandise" before he steals regular priced items. Adherence to the following paragraphs may keep another from grief: Employes may not give, receive, or take for themselves any "As Is" merchandise, samples, discarded equipment, parts, or supplies. This procedure provides a method for selling such goods to employes. Prices charged should be reasonable in relation to the value of the goods. . . .

Signed _____ Protection.

Information such as the following is a helpful reminder:

PROTECTION REPORT #____

An employe carried a large package with a one $ salescheck from the drug section applied as a pass-out. Because one $ would not purchase drugs of that volume the package was inspected. It contained merchandise valued at $22.50 in addition to the one $'s worth of drugs. This incident enabled Protection to learn of other thefts this employe had committed.

A package being delivered to her home was intercepted. It contained merchandise with a retail value of $582.25 but the salescheck was for "1 lot of remnants 82¢ net." The price was authorized by an approved signature.

The employe was reluctant to accept all the blame. She felt, and perhaps with some justification, that part of the responsibility rested with the supervisor who authorized the unitemized salescheck, and then delivered the shipper to her in the stockroom, without looking at the merchandise that she had assembled.

In previous programs the statement has been made, "often the little, or seemingly unimportant things, if investigated, will help to reduce shrinkage." It certainly would have applied in this case.

Signed _____ Protection.

For a different approach to the suggestion program we distributed reprints of an article published in *Business Week*. The article pictured a man wearing pants that were much too large around the waist and he was photographed demonstrating how stolen merchandise could be concealed in his too large trousers. The article was appropriate because of a current theft attempt.

PROTECTION REPORT #____

We thought you might be interested in the attached article:[1]

We were, because the magazine in which it appeared arrived in Protection simultaneously with a loss report from the men's coat section.

"SIZE OF THE TAKE"

Just how much profit disappears into a booster's oversize pants _____?

---

[1] Cracking Down On Shoplifters, *Business Week*, November 1, 1952. Reprints from McGraw-Hill Publishing Co., Inc.

The "Roomy Pants" are not a fantasy. An alert salesman reported to his section manager that a man had stolen an overcoat. The manager could not determine from the man's appearance that he had the coat, but did follow him down the stairway in the hopes of being able to point him out to an operator. On the way down, the man pulled an overcoat from his trousers and threw it on the stairs.

What profit had disappeared into his pants? The coat that was recovered was priced at $465.

The shoplifter was accompanied by another man, and while we do not expect them to return to the same section soon, they no doubt will "boost" in other parts of the store.

The finding of our investigation may help you.

The price ticket on the recovered coat had a pencil notation —$465 written just above the printed price. Several other garments were found to have the same pencil notation written just above the printed price. These pencil prices were not made officially by any employe. We are sure they were made by someone to indicate, to the boosters, the merchandise to be stolen. Please notify us of any price tickets found in your section, that have the selling price repeated in pencil on the price ticket.

The "Roomy Pants" are not the only enlightening feature of the article. We recommend the complete article for interesting reading.

Signed _____ Protection.

There is no limit to the possibilities for reporting loss methods to supervisors. One store prepared novel circulars, with a variety of caricatures, which were placed on supervisors' desks before the store opened.

The Willmark Service System, Inc., have published pamphlets designed to be instructive to both executives and salespeople. Two that are informative for salespeople are: "an EYE on the shoplifter" and "cash across the counter!"

Willmark Pioneer" directed to executives included: "Pefect Inventory Covers Up $7580 Theft"; "Rubbish Collector Guilty, $4200 Inventory Shortage"; and "$19,000 Refund Fraud Discovered, Executive Assistant Confesses."

Supplied for Salespeople by Willmark Service System, Inc.

Another pre-holiday report might be:

PROTECTION REPORT #____

Thefts of all kinds reach their peak during the next few weeks and certainly a large portion of our yearly shrinkage is accumulated during this period.

A reminder of some of the causes, and a few suggestions, may help you and your assistants to maintain a satisfactory shrinkage for the year. Be alert to "Confidence Games":

A vigilant sponsor in one section overheard a man tell a salesperson, "Take your money and come with me." The sponsor interrupted and the man said he was taking the intended victim to Mr. Delehan's office. To the question, "By what authority?" he said, "call 287 they will tell you." He disappeared while a call was made to Protection. We appreciate this sponsor's keen

Suggested Brochures and Reports 235

perception. We had no Mr. Delehan and no phone 287. The same trick was tried at two other stores. In one he accompanied an assistant Section Manager and salesperson to the cash division and after instructing them to sit down while he took the money into the cage for the "Treasury Men" to check for counterfeits, he walked off with the money.

This is just one version of "Con-Game." At the present we are looking for the culprit. If a person of the following description contacts you, phone _____:

> Man—white—early 20's—5'5" to 5'8", short, black and shiny wavy hair combed straight back, dark complexion, wearing salt and pepper tweed topcoat, very full cut, no hat, has cold sore on lip.

Last Saturday a man was apprehended after he had stolen $200 worth of merchandise from a stockroom area. He was sentenced to one year in the House of Correction; however, there are others after boxed merchandise. They may pass as employes; strict vigilance is our only defense.

One narcotic addict has been seen several times the past few days. If seen looking at boxed merchandise in out of the way places, phone _____. His description:

> Man—medium dark—21 years—5'11"—150 lbs. nervous twitch around mouth and nose.

Refunds are still being given on merchandise which has either been stolen or purchased fraudulently on charge accounts.

Twelve items of a kind were purchased in August, by one section, and soon sold out; then the same item began to come back on credit, six of them in a few days, which caused the section to investigate and discover that both the upper and lower portion of a cash register check were used, on different days, to obtain refunds on the same merchandise. The manufacturer has reported losses of the article from his stock and it may develop that his shortage is responsible for our returns.

Enforcement of employe rules is especially important during the next few weeks.

A police official states he can recognize the December pickpocket file by the thickness of the folder. Pick-pockets work wherever there are crowds. Their methods vary very little because they are based upon the simple acts of distraction and extraction. There are distractions because of crowds, and jostling is fundamental to the extraction.

Shoplifters also increase their activities because employes are kept busy.

You will remember that our chart showing arrests went over the top in December.

Signed _____ Protection

The periodical notices should aim at stating current problems, reviewing rules and procedures, and emphasizing that the supervisor is the key factor in shrinkage reduction.

Chapter 30
INTERNAL CONTROL

OPPORTUNITIES to steal can be controlled. Seldom does a defrauder develop an original idea in his peculations. Similar methods are used and have been used for many years. The defrauder who dips his hands into the cash drawer, without manipulating the records, is like a pickpocket or shoplifter. When the embezzler attempts to cover his tracks by manipulation, his attempt at concealment may delay exposure of his thefts.

It is not my intention to dwell on accounting methods; however some mention of Internal Control is made because the embezzler, on the payroll, knows how to commit frauds, but many business men do not know how to protect themselves against it. Every possible precaution should be taken for protection. The insurance indemnity offered by fidelity bond coverage should only be considered as supplemental protection.

Accounting systems and internal control procedures depend upon the size of the business. An owner of a small store, who handles his own accounting, can control his business. As soon as it becomes large enough to require employes to handle the assets, controls are required.

Larger stores maintain the services of auditing firms that will discover weaknesses in the accounting systems. The accountants will, no doubt, in addition to verifying the accounting figures, check the taking of inventory for exactness and set up periodical physical cash counts. They will verify bank balances, accounts receivable and audit accounts payable.

The internal audit or control departments, of stores, also have the duty of constant supervision to insure that controls are not breaking down.

Inventory control is of great importance, especially the actual count while taking the official inventory. Section personnel have falsified inventory records and the statement was made by one lecturer, at a comptroller's meeting, that "three key individuals had manipulated inventory so that instead of 1.3 per cent shrinkage over a period of five years, it should have been 24 per cent."

Printed, numerical, forms have advantage for internal control. If consideration is given to the elimination of them in the interest of expeditiousness, or work simplification, other types of control—mechanical or other—should be substituted.

Embezzlements of refunds, once started, usually continue and grow until the embezzler becomes careless and exposes himself. Some of these frauds have run into many thousands of dollars before being uncovered. A periodical review of the controls of refunds is advisable. Systems will break down if disregarded.

Authorization signatures have frequently been forged. A current file should be maintained of all authorized signatures and all forms requiring an authorization should, at least, be spot checked. Any variation in signatures should be investigated.

Adjustments, or allowances to customers, have been the downfall of many people working in those departments. The loss or adjustment accounts should be constantly reviewed for any major increases.

The customers shortage accounts for one mail order firm ran high and was accepted as a calculated loss for conducting the business. No concerted effort was made to find the cause, and reduce it, until the protection personnel became concerned with the loss of guns. Their investigation was responsible for reducing this loss account by about $100,000 a year in succeeding years.

Customers always claimed non-delivery of goods but every fall claims for guns ran fifteen to twenty a week. They were scattered over the country and delivery systems were by various means of transportation.

A controlled operation for guns was instituted. They were checked from the time of receipt until they reached the shipping dock which was used by postal trucks and by other carriers. The control indicated that further investigation of the dock was required and a night time check of it disclosed postal labels which had been removed from packages.

Surveillance of the personnel indicated that the supervisor personally loaded certain trucks, and when he was seen to load guns, the truck was followed and the drop off point located. A change in the shipping platform personnel effected the extraordinary reduction in the customers allowance account.

The control of timekeeping and payroll are important, especially where day help or part time workers are used, and when overtime is prevalent.

Receiving, handling, and disbursing of incoming mail is an extremely important part of doing business, especially if cash is likely to be received. Controls should be adequate to insure safety.

C.O.D. collections are a hazard. Drivers have failed to turn in receipts and they have also "borrowed" the collection for a few days, then turned it in on a pay-day. C.O.D. packages have been stolen and delivered by the thief who kept the proceeds. C.O.D. record systems should prevent embezzlement.

Cash disbursement vouchers and remittances to customers are a risk. One man found that he could secure signature authorization to obtain checks in payment of trucking bills. He associated with a business man who would cash them for him and later he would pass a regular invoice for payment to the trucking company, through regular channels.

Cycle billing of account receivables can be manipulated. Employes of billing departments have thrown away sales checks and one report was that a woman had twenty-three of her friends open accounts. She carried a Bible daily and placed the checks for their accounts in it, to carry out.

Both the receiving and shipping of merchandise need to be controlled and persons handling either should not have access to the accounts payable or receivable records.

In order to prevent the embezzlement from cash registers, all shortages should be investigated. Borrowing from cash funds may lead to more serious thefts. A cash audit should include the checking of banks assigned to salespeople.

Petty cash should be accounted for. The very name belittles the importance of it and some employes have made a practice of pilfering from it; also from postage funds or supplies.

Expense accounts, and car allowances should require supervision because they are a source of fraud on occasions.

Fraud or embezzlement is a problem for each individual store.

No two companies are exactly alike, even though systems required are similar. This can only be a guide as to where and how safeguards and preventive measures should be erected.

It is not alone important to attack loss and waste because of economic consequences, but also because it is wrong—morally wrong. According to the statistics, controls cause fifty per cent of the population to remain honest.

Chapter 31
SHRINKAGE PREVENTION—SUMMARY

THE PUBLISHED average national shrinkage, or stock shortage, for all of the reporting stores, has been somewhat over one per cent to sales for a period of years.

Some stores have kept shrinkage under one per cent; others, even stores with established protection departments, suffer a shrinkage considerably in excess of the one per cent. Shrinkage for some stores has run as high as two and a half per cent of sales, or even higher.

Based on the average shrinkage percentage, it is not difficult to accept the fantastic estimates, that have been published, of the total losses of all retailers throughout the country. A store having total sales of one million dollars a year could expect a shrinkage of ten thousand dollars; sales of fifty million might result in a shrinkage of five hundred thousand dollars; and with a total sales of one hundred million a loss figure in excess of one million dollars would not be unusual.

The only perplexing feature of the staggering loss to retailers is that a greater effort is not made by many store owners and managements to reduce or prevent it.

Some individual stores have been successful with cooperative shrinkage reduction programs. Some merchants' associations have sponsored clinics to study the problem of loss, and in some cities the merchants have associated with the local law enforcement agencies to conduct a theft prevention drive. Benefits have no doubt been gained from every effort, but shrinkage is a never ending problem; therefore, it is one that should rate top priority with every store owner, merchant, or management team, every year.

I have shown how professional shoplifters, or boosters, have been practicing thefts against merchants for centuries. Automobiles have made it possible for today's professional boosters to perform their trade in remote areas as well as in the shopping centers of cities.

The increase in narcotic addiction in recent years has increased potential shoplifters by the thousands. A user becomes a confirmed addict within a matter of weeks, and the requirements to satisfy his craving may run from $20 to $70, or more, per day. In the majority of cases, these funds can be obtained only through crime. Boosting is the answer for many addicts.

In numbers of persons who shoplift, the non-professional, or amateurs, outnumbered those who pursue the trade as a career. If not apprehended soon after starting a shoplifting career, these people may become habitual boosters from habit. They are people who have yielded to temptation, or are suffering from some anxiety or emotional instability, or physical disturbance. They may come from any family, profession, trade, or social group.

The immaturity of youth leads many of our juveniles and adolescents to become a problem to merchants.

Merchants not only have to face security problems with the public, but employes are an additional risk.

Employes are recruited from the public. They are people with the same weaknesses and yield to the same temptations; therefore, they create the same problems—only greater—because of the many more opportunities they have to defraud the employer.

Every attempt should be made, prior to employment, to screen out those persons who are naturally dishonest. Screening of prospective employes is necessary because unscrupulous individuals do attempt to secure employment in stores and members of organized gangs have operated as store employes.

One professional shoplifter from another city once stated, "I travel all over the country because I get the urge, and it is profitable." She then boasted that in her home town she got everything she wanted without going near the stores. She claimed that she and her gang have people working for them in practically every stockroom, and that organized gang runners visit the employe, especially on lunch hours, pick up packages and deliver them to a fence. Both runners and the employes are paid a set amount per trip.

Shrinkage Prevention—Summary

Many employes will remain honest no matter how strong the temptation. Some employes will remain honest because of the efficiency of the systems, controls, and supervision. Some employes will yield to temptation.

The very nature and scope of a retail business warrants the training of all employes to think in terms of theft and shrinkage prevention, not only when dealing with the public, but also in their own actions.

Cash in the bank is protected by automatic alarm systems and uniformed, armed guards. It is secured in vaults at night and protected by time locks. The tellers are balanced daily and the books checked periodically by auditors and examiners. With these precautions, one reads of bank employes being arrested who have tried to beat the systems.

Merchandise in a store is the equivalent of cash in the bank, yet it cannot be secured in the same manner. Neither the small storekeeper, nor the large department store has the detailed elaborate physical and financial safeguards that banks possess to protect cash. Insurance is not the answer to merchant's pilferage.

What is the answer, and who is responsible for the protection of the assets of a merchant?

In the small store, the owner or manager is responsible for watching his assets, but he should be aware of the problems and hazards he faces.

The larger organization must depend on the supervisors to motivate all employes to protect the assets.

The accounting division may control the procedures designed to protect and safeguard the company's assets. These control procedures are very necessary for the success of the business, just as employe rules are necessary, but neither the procedures nor the rules will be effective in protecting the assets unless they are enforced.

The inventory control division may coordinate the efforts of all sections in order to obtain accurate results; audit all procedures which affect the control of inventories; issue instructions, and supervise the physical taking of inventories; arrange for and supervise the calculations for obtaining the final inventory results. They then can investigate the causes of abnormally large shortages and overages and ferret out errors that may be responsible.

If the inventory control personnel cannot account for shrinkage, the problem can be passed on to the protection department to try and determine if it has been caused by theft.

Now—who is responsible for supervision and enforcement of the rules and procedures that have been established to protect the assets? It is the section manager and his assistants, because he is responsible for his section's merchandise inventory. That means that he is directly responsible for his shrinkage figure, which means that he and his supervisory assistants are responsible for:

> Supervising control procedures
> Enforcing employe rules
> Maintaining special checks and inspections
> Reporting of all thefts or suspicions
> Employe education for shrinkage reduction

In order to accomplish his responsibilities, the section manager should have the cooperation of management, the personnel, training, accounting, inventory control, operating and the protection divisions, but most of all, he should be trained in protection and alerted to the risks and perils facing all merchants.

Occasionally a section manager or assistant may deliberately falsify some records, in order to cover up some failure and to improve his profit contribution.

Quoting one merchandise manager:

> The results of my sections have been right on the button for a number of years because all markdowns are taken. I may have an argument with management over the amount of my markdowns, but I don't have a large shrinkage to account for. If we encounter a bad season the necessary markdowns are taken and we go on from there.

The buyers reporting to this man verify his statement. Markdown books are available, so that every entry is made promptly, for any repricing of any merchandise.

In my opinion, another reason for his satisfactory shrinkage

Shrinkage Prevention—Summary

is the fact that a buyer or an assistant is on the selling floor supervising the employes in each of his sections every hour of the day. Each one of his supervisory assistants knows what is expected of him and follows the example he sets.

Price changes or other accounting records made in memorandum form or carried in the mind often fail to be recorded, thus causing accounting discrepancies.

The auditing of inventory listings is important in preventing deliberate fraud. A spot count taken by a representative of the auditing firm during inventory did not tally with the inventory books. A further check indicated that a number of listings had been altered. Investigation developed the fact that a section assistant had made the alterations after the inventory listings were completed, and before they were turned over to the accounting office.

The first explanation of the man, who altered the figures, was that he wanted his section manager to have a good showing. He later admitted the reason for adding to the inventory was to cover up his thefts and special prices given to friends without taking markdowns.

If a company maintains a protection department, a protection policy has no doubt been formulated. I recommend that stores and companies who do not have a department devoted to protection establish a policy aimed at theft prevention. If shoplifters are to be arrested, the personnel assigned the responsibility should be well trained so that no mistake is made. They should be indoctrinated in the procedure to be followed before and after an arrest.

Help should be obtained in policy decisions from the firm's legal advisors. Local law enforcement agencies or trade associations may also be helpful. The protection personnel of the larger stores may be able and willing to advise smaller stores on policy decisions.

A protection policy should include the action to be taken in case of employe thefts. The action taken should be consistent in every case. Benefits are lost if one employe is fired for stealing and another given a second chance. The principle is important rather than the amount stolen.

A "Conference Board Report"[1] recommends that industrial theft control programs must put more emphasis on prevention of thefts, and one of their specific recommendations is that supervision be alerted to the problems.

A store supervisor cannot be on the scene to spot each theft or fraud, nor every error, but spot checks and periodical inspections by all supervisors will accomplish two important things:

1. Emphasize the importance of the enforcement of rules and procedures.
2. Eventually disclose violations.

By setting a high standard a manager will likely reduce his shrinkage. Section personnel quickly recognize a model and are often proud of an admirable one. One salesperson who had worked in several departments once said, "Sections in the store are not all operated as though they are part of the same organization. I love this section. The buyer is considerate, and she is *so correct* in everything she does—every little detail. Some of the things I have seen in other departments are not the same."

The cooperation of all personnel is indispensable to success. Often the little or seemingly unimportant things, if investigated, will help to promote a shrinking shrinkage.

[1] Theft Control Procedures. Highlights for the Executive. Conference Board Reports. Industrial Security III. *Studies in Business Policy No. 70.* National Industrial Conference Board, Inc., New York, 1954.

Chapter 32
MATERIAL FOR FURTHER STUDY OF PROTECTION

A STUDY of protection and stock shortage control, for retailers, can be just as exciting as a career in merchandising. It could include a study of criminology and accounting, both of which are a profession in themselves.

I have tried to give an intimate account of the problems encountered, in order to stress the importance of control, for both small and large stores.

The merchant whose duties include those of buyer, sales, advertising, and personnel manager, yet has the responsibility for protection and shrinkage control, may be interested in other helpful publications.

A study of methods and procedures to reduce inventory losses, *Stock Shortage Control Manual,* was published by the National Retail Dry Goods Association, Controllers' Congress (now The National Retail Merchants Association).

The proceedings of a "Clinic On Shoplifting and Other Store Protection Problems" contained helpful information. It was available at the Chicago Retail Merchants Association.

A *Manual for Store Protection* contains a non-technical discussion of the law and of legal problems a store protection agent will encounter in the course of his duties. This booklet, available from The Retail Special Service Association, Inc., Chicago, may be of interest to retailers, even those located outside of Illinois. It could be used as a guide in discussing local laws with regional law enforcement agencies or legal advisors.

The *Manual for Store Protection,* by Fred E. Inbau, Professor of Law, Northwestern University, prepared for and published by The Retail Special Service Association, Inc., covers specific subjects:

    I. The Law of Arrest, Search, and Seizure

II. The Right to Detain and Question Suspected Employes
III. The Right to Eject and to Arrest Persons Who Abuse Their Privileges as Invited Customers
IV. The Right to Regain or Retake Possession of Store Property
V. Crimes and Criminal Law Principles of Particular Importance to Store Protection Agents
VI. Criminal Procedures
VII. The Courts of Chicago, Cook County, and Illinois
VIII. Preparing a Case for Trial

Shoplifting And The Law Of Arrest: The Merchant's Dilemma, by Jon R. Waltz, was available as a reprint from the *Yale Law Journal,* Volume 62, Number 5, April 1953. This is a concise treatise on the subject and it gives 125 footnote references to legal decisions of various courts, comments of law enforcement personnel, magazine articles, and books dealing with the subject. It should be helpful to legal advisors.

I have purposely refrained from advising when or how to make an arrest. A *Manual on Criminal Law and Procedure,* by Professor Ernst W. Puttkammer, published by the Chicago Crime Commission was available for the benefit of Illinois police officers. There are, no doubt, similar references on the subject of criminal law procedures in other states.

Forgery and Fictitious Checks, by Julius L. Sternitzky, Inspector (Retired) Oakland Police Department, Charles C Thomas, Publisher, Springfield, Illinois, exposed the methods used by crooks in forging and passing fictitious checks.

I have used the services of a polygraph or lie-detector operator, in investigations, intermittently for twenty years. Inquiries have been received from many stores regarding the use of the technique. *Lie Detection and Criminal Interrogation* (3d ed., 1953), by Fred E. Inbau, Professor of Law, Northwestern University, Former Director, Chicago Police Scientific Crime Detection Laboratory, and John E. Reid, Director, John E. Reid and Associates, former Staff Member, Chicago Police Scientific Crime Detection Laboratory, publisher, The Williams & Wilkins Company, Baltimore, covers "The Lie Detector Technique" and "Criminal Interrogation."

Further Study of Protection

The storekeeper interested in the story of *The Professional Thief*, who had been engaged in that profession for more than twenty years, will find the book by the same name enlightening. It is *By A Professional Thief*, annotated and interpreted by Edwin H. Sutherland, Sociology Department, Indiana University, published by The University of Chicago Press, Chicago, Illinois.

This professional thief describes a "booster" as a professional thief who will ask a salesman for some article and then steal what he wants from other accessible articles. He describes a "heel" as a sneak thief who steals without asking for assistance of a salesman. The method used by the "heel" in men's clothing departments is described. While the "heel" may ignore the greeter in the department and walk past him, on the way in, as though he has the most important business of anyone in the store, he may engage him in conversation on the way out with a stolen overcoat over his arm. The footnote on page 50 describes how one young man operated, and was apprehended by a detective because a salesman in the department had a special interest in catching thieves. I recognize the incident, the salesman, and the detective involved.

I take exception to the authenticity of the footnote, on page 49, of the book. It relates a tale that I have heard figuratively hundreds of times, but have never been able to verify. Each time the story is told it relates to a woman personally known to someone who passed it on. It relates that a Chicago department store made a present of a mink coat to a woman whom they had accused of stealing a compact which she proved she had purchased from another store.

Interrogation of thieves is most successful when handled properly. Information to assist in preventing further thefts or reducing shrinkage can often be obtained from a person already apprehended. Chapters on "Interrogations" and "Admissions, Confessions, and Written Statements," in *Fundamentals of Criminal Investigations*, will benefit the individual making a career of store protection. The author is Charles E. O'Hara, Lecturer in Police Science, Western Reserve University, Cleveland, Ohio, Charles C Thomas, Publisher, Springfield, Illinois.

250   Shoplifting and Shrinkage Protection

Good advice for anyone likely to be held up is contained in: *Armed Robbery—A Manual for Persons Likely to be Held Up*, by Richard L. Holcomb, Associate Professor of Public Affairs, Bureau of Public Affairs, State University of Iowa, Iowa City, Iowa.

Criminology and Crime Prevention, by Lois Lundell Higgins, Director, Crime Prevention Bureau of Illinois, and Edward A. Fitzpatrick, President Emeritus, Mount Mary College, Director, Institute of Human Education, The Bruce Publishing Company, Milwaukee, has for its aim: "A germinal knowledge, a live knowledge, an energized knowledge for student, police officer, parent, and citizen."

A book that should be of especial interest to those persons responsible for guards or watchmen in store property is: *Industrial Plant Protection,* by John Richelieu Davis, Lecturer in Industrial Security, Michigan State University, Charles C Thomas, Publisher, Springfield, Illinois. This is a comprehensive book on plant protection and safety.

Any reference I have made to the law is only incidental, not a specific recommendation to be followed by anyone unaware of its application in his jurisdiction. I do suggest that any legal questions involved, in arriving at a protection problem, be interpreted by a counselor.

An article that could be extremely helpful in determining a protection policy, and be beneficial to legal advisors is, *The Protection and Recapture of Merchandise from Shoplifters;* it contains excellent advice to the merchant untrained in the art of making arrests. For the lawyer, there are 75 footnotes referring to court decisions, mainly on false arrest or imprisonment, assault and battery, slander, etc.

In conclusion, and to stress the need for caution in making arrests, I quote from the aforementioned article:[1]

> The shoplifter and the suspected shoplifter have been and will continue to be an expensive nuisance to merchants, and a prolific source of litigation. Unless the merchant can afford to

[1] "The Protection and Recapture of Merchandise from Shoplifters," Vol. 46, No. 6, 1952, *Illinois Law Review* (1952), and Vol. 47, No. 1, 1952, *Northwestern University Law Review*. Reprinted by special permission.

hire a skilled corps of private detectives to guard his stock, he stands to lose unknown sums either in stolen goods, legal judgments, or both. Relatively few cases arise involving acts by trained professional detectives, but in these days of high wages, the cost is prohibitive to many merchants. "The employe who is likely to get his employer in legal trouble is usually a manager or assistant manager, with authority to act generally but untrained in the law of larceny, unskilled in the art of quiet apprehension and too busy with his primary duties to follow and observe a suspected shoplifter until the case against him is secure. Too often this type of employe acts on partial information or mere suspicion and makes costly mistakes."